SAME-SEX MARRIAGE

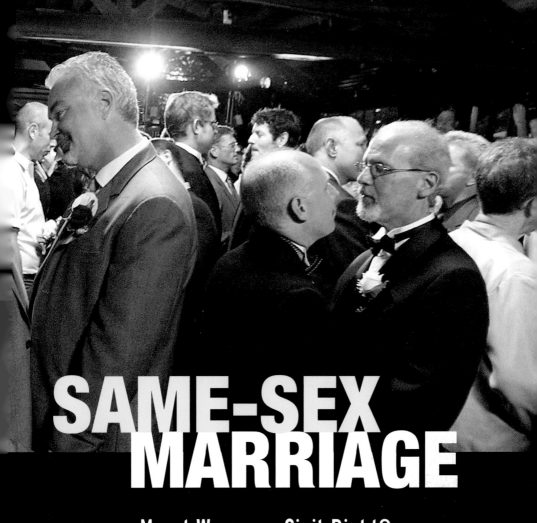

SAME-SEX
MARRIAGE

Moral Wrong or Civil Right?

TRICIA ANDRYSZEWSKI

Twenty-First Century Books
A division of Lerner Publishing Group, Inc.
241 First Avenue North
Minneapolis, MN 55401 U.S.A.

Website address: www.lernerbooks.com

Library of Congress Cataloging-in-Publication Data

Andryszewski, Tricia, 1956–
    Same-sex marriage / by Tricia Andryszewski.
      p. cm.
    Includes bibliographical references and index.
    ISBN 978-0-8225-7176-6 (lib bdg. : alk. paper)
      1. Same-sex marriage—United States. 2. Same-sex marriage—Law and legislation—United States. 3. Gay rights—United States. I. Title.
    HQ1034.U5A53 2008
    306.84′80973—dc22   2007010397

Manufactured in the United States of America
1 2 3 4 5 6 – PA – 13 12 11 10 09 08

CONTENTS

INTRODUCTION

Ray Boylan and his partner Stanley Wilson invited family and friends to witness their commitment ceremony in 1996. "We felt it was really important for our families to understand our seriousness, that we aren't just promiscuous party boys," Ray recalls. "We, like other people, feel that a ceremony gives others a familiar context for understanding what's happening right before their eyes. How else would Stanley ever agree to kiss me in front of his mother? . . .

"Yes, we would get married legally if we could. . . . Like any couple we negotiate our issues and deal with our conflicts. But it's a comfort knowing we've been committed and cannot get out—we have witnesses." Seven years after their commitment ceremony, Ray and Stanley were legally married in Massachusetts.

In the United States, marriage is both a religious experience and a legal, civil contract. Many churches in recent years have blessed the unions of homosexual members—marriage between two people of the same sex. Even among religious groups most opposed to homosexuality (sexual attraction to members of the same

Maxine Kincora (left) and Jan Safford (right) were married on March 25, 1996, in a civil-union ceremony in San Francisco, California. California does not recognize same-sex marriage.

7

sex), a few of their clergy have blessed such unions. In addition, many couples have had nonreligious commitment ceremonies. In these ceremonies, both partners typically pledge to love, honor, and care for each other.

But meaningful as each of these same-sex ceremonies has been to its participants, none was legally binding anywhere in the United States until 2004. Then Massachusetts began to allow same-sex marriage for residents of that state. However, those Massachusetts same-sex marriages are not legally recognized by the U.S. government or by most other states. Ironically, churches, which typically require those they will marry to undergo classes, counseling, and confessions of faith, have been more willing to marry homosexual couples than the government. Unlike churches, the state treats marriage for heterosexuals as a fundamental civil right and imposes no such requirements.

Legal marriage brings with it serious obligations—and significant benefits. These can include spousal health insurance, shared retirement benefits, tax advantages, various inheritance rights, and family rates on everything from swimming pool passes to auto insurance. Legal marriage also carries the intangible but very important benefit of conveying to the world that the couple involved is truly a family.

OPINION MAKER

"We are not seeking special treatment. We seek equality. We are asking that marriage laws be applied equally to all couples, regardless of sexual orientation. That is the only gay agenda—equality for everyone under the law."

—THE REVEREND TROY PERRY, METROPOLITAN COMMUNITY CHURCH (A CHURCH SPECIFICALLY DEDICATED TO MINISTERING TO GAY MEN AND LESBIANS) LOS ANGELES, CALIFORNIA, N.D.

Pictured here in 2003 are Olivier du Wulf *(left)* with his son, Laurent, and du Wulf's partner, Steven Boulliane *(right),* with his son, Patrice, in San Francisco. Without legally recognized same-sex marriage, families such as these don't enjoy the same legal benefits as families with heterosexual parents.

Unable to be legally married, same-sex couples pursuing a committed relationship must piece together a host of protections and sharing arrangements. These arrangements are either automatic or far simpler for legally married couples. Such legal measures range from wills to joint property ownership to name changes. Making these arrangements often requires the costly help of lawyers and accountants. It is true that many corporations and some local governments have extended spousal benefits to the unmarried domestic partners (homosexual and heterosexual) of their employees. But some protections and benefits are simply unavailable to same-sex couples.

Antigay activists believe that this is as it should be. They believe that marriage and its benefits should be reserved for heterosexual couples. These activists believe that God intended it to

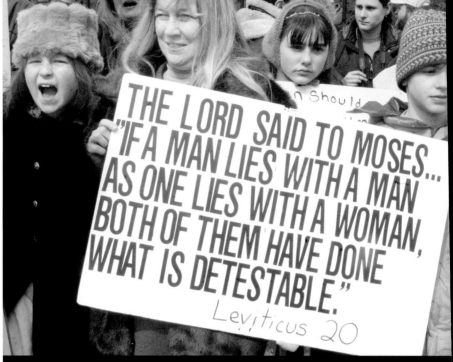

A crowd gathered outside the Massachusetts State House of Representatives to protest same-sex marriage as the state legislature was debating the issue in March 2004. Anti-gay activists frequently use passages from the Bible to justify their message that marriage should be between a man and a woman.

be that way and that reserving marriage for heterosexuals furthers society's interest in encouraging stable, traditional, child-bearing families.

Gay-rights activists counter that marriage is a civil right as well as a religious rite. They say that all they are asking for is the same legal status currently available to heterosexual

OPINION MAKER

"Affirming same-sex marriage would forever alter the meaning of marriage and family for everyone."

—GLENN T. STANTON AND BILL MAIER, FOCUS ON THE FAMILY, A CONSERVATIVE RELIGIOUS GROUP, 2004 couples, whether they be atheists, sterile, or religiously observant and childbearing. In addition, gay-rights activists contend that society's interest in stable families would be furthered still more by supporting stable homosexual families as it supports traditional heterosexual families. "Given the fact that we already allow legal gay relationships," gay conservative Andrew Sullivan writes, "what possible social goal is advanced by framing the law to encourage those relationships to be unfaithful, undeveloped, and insecure?"

Clearly, many Americans disapprove of homosexual sex. But the vast majority of Americans believes that everyone, homosexual as well as heterosexual, deserves a basic level of civil rights protection. Exactly what should be included in that package of civil rights—and, in particular, whether the right to marry should be included—is likely to be debated well into the twenty-first century.

CHAPTER ONE

The Background: Gay Rights in the United States

At three o'clock on the morning of June 28, 1969, New York City police raided the Stonewall Inn, a bar catering to homosexuals. The raid itself was not unusual. Police often targeted such bars and harassed their patrons. But what followed was very unusual. Instead of passively allowing the police to shut the bar down, as in the past, the bar's patrons and sympathizers from the neigh-borhood fought back. They threw trash at the police and rioted for nearly an hour.

For several nights, crowds gathered to protest the Stonewall raid, clashing with police. Over the next few weeks, the riots were followed by larger, more peaceful protest rallies.

The Stonewall riots were a turning point in the way homosexuality was perceived and treated in the United States. Before Stonewall, homosexual sex was illegal in every state except Illinois. (Not until 2003 did the U.S. Supreme Court declare laws against sodomy

In 1969 patrons resisted a police raid at the Stonewall Inn, a bar in New York City that catered to gay men. The event marked a turning point in the history of gay and lesbian life in the United States.

[anal or oral sex] to be unconstitutional. By then, only about one-third of the states had such laws in force.) Known homosexuals were banned from many professions, including teaching, law, medicine, the armed forces—and even hairdressing in many states. And no law or public policy protected homosexuals from discrimination in jobs, housing, or public accommodations such as restaurants and hotels.

Stonewall both marked and inspired a growing new openness about sexual orientation. But the gay-rights movement didn't just suddenly appear after the Stonewall raid. Homosexuality has been a fact of life throughout human history. Sometimes it has been tolerated. Occasionally it has been celebrated. But most often, it has been condemned. In the mid-1960s, inspired by the successes of the black civil rights movement, groups of gay men and lesbians (female homosexuals) began to fight discrimination. Meanwhile, a general climate of tolerance, permissiveness, and sexual openness swept the country. As part of this change, various mainstream U.S. organizations announced their opposition to laws against homosexual sex and other forms of discrimination against homosexuals. These groups included the American Civil Liberties Union in 1967, the American Sociological Association in 1969, the Lutheran Church in 1970, and the American Bar Association in 1973.

GAY LIBERATION

The new burst of gay-rights activism ushered in by Stonewall was closely related to other protest and youth liberation movements of the time. The antiwar, black power, and women's liberation movements were also taking off. Like the other movements, gay liberation was often flamboyant, in your face, and outrageous. This "gay liberation" phase of the gay-rights movement focused more on personal liberation than civil rights. The movement insisted that "gay is good" and that homosexuals should accept their homosexuality and "come out," acknowledging it openly.

Many of the gay men and lesbians intent on "liberation" in the early 1970s rejected the very idea of marriage as "heterosexist." Marriage, according to this way of thinking, was an outdated institution that oppressed women by enforcing sex roles inappropriate for homosexuals. Still, in the 1970s, gay activists held diverse ideas. Many sought the right to marry even then. A few demanded and were refused marriage licenses. Others were married in religious or other ceremonies not recognized as legally valid.

Gay liberation dominated the gay-rights movement from 1969 through the early 1970s. In 1970 a gay pride parade in New York City drew about ten thousand marchers. By the end of the following year, gay liberation groups had sprung up in just about every large city and college campus across the United States.

Participants rally at the nation's first gay pride march down Christopher Street in the Greenwich Village neighborhood in New York City on June 28, 1970. The event marked the one-year anniversary of the raid on Stonewall Inn.

One notable success of the gay liberationists was their challenge to the American medical establishment's view of homosexuality. For much of the twentieth century, doctors considered homosexuality to be a kind of disease. In 1974, after a sustained campaign of protest and pressure, the American Psychiatric Association removed homosexuality from its list of medical diseases and disorders. The modern-day consensus among U.S. medical authorities is that homosexual orientation is an unchangeable characteristic. It is established either before birth or in very early childhood.

Gay liberation had widespread effects even for gay men and lesbians who never joined a protest march. With more homosexuals in the public eye, gay pride and self-acceptance became easier. Sizable, highly visible homosexual communities gathered in

Barbara Gittings (right) was a prominent gay-rights activist. She lobbied the American Psychiatric Association (APA) to change its stance on homosexuality as a mental disorder. In 1973 the APA removed sexual orientation from its list of mental disorders. She is shown here protesting the federal government's discrimination in hiring based on sexual orientation.

During the gay liberation movement, homosexuals across the United States became more visible and more vocal about equal rights. *Above:* Marchers in San Francisco, California, held their own gay pride parade in June 1970 on the one-year anniversary of the Stonewall Inn raid.

cities around the nation. Those cities included San Francisco, New York, Chicago, Houston, Miami, Philadelphia, Seattle, and elsewhere. Greater homosexual visibility fueled the growth of a new, chiefly male marketplace of bars, discos, and vacation destinations, as well as doctors, lawyers, and other service providers catering to a homosexual clientele.

The cultural unrest that gave rise to gay liberation groups subsided in the mid-1970s. But the push for gay rights didn't fade away. Instead, it became increasingly visible. Established, organized gay and lesbian communities shifted toward seeking political and legal reforms. They also sought full acceptance in the workplace, in housing, and in such mainstream institutions as churches.

Beginning in 1974, liberal representatives repeatedly proposed amending the Civil Rights Act to extend federal protection against discrimination to homosexuals. Congress rejected the proposals. Gay-rights activists were blocked at the federal level. But they had more success at the state and local level. By the late 1970s, several dozen local communities had adopted some form of protection against discrimination for homosexuals. Most of these communities were university towns, as well as a few large cities (Detroit, Minneapolis, San Francisco, Seattle, and Washington, D.C.) with organized gay and lesbian communities.

Much of the U.S. public seemed ready to accept at least some such change. As early as 1977, more than half believed that homosexuals should have equal rights in job opportunities. Only a third believed that they shouldn't.

BACKLASH

However, in the late 1970s, a widely publicized backlash emerged against homosexuality in general and gay rights in particular. A small minority passionately opposed to homosexuality began to compete with gay-rights activists for the hearts and votes of the vast number of Americans who had never given much thought to the matter. This competitive struggle has continued ever since.

Singer Anita Bryant founded a crusade against a gay-rights ordinance in Miami, Florida, on February 15, 1977. She founded an antigay group called Save Our Children.

Gay-rights laws indicate how widespread the debate had become. By the mid-1980s, dozens of U.S. cities and several states had included sexual orientation in local and state human rights measures. Typically, this was done by adding "sexual orientation" to a list of categories against which discrimination is prohibited by civil rights law. Such measure might, for example, ban a local government from discriminating on the basis of race, religion, national origin, handicapped status, or sexual preference when hiring employees or providing services. Some measures prohibited private citizens as well as government from discriminating in such activities as renting an apartment, hiring an employee, serving customers in a restaurant, or providing other forms of "public accommodation."

The march did not progress steadily in one direction, though. Antigay-rights activists successfully fought to defeat or repeal gay-rights measures in dozens of communities. They also proposed—and some communities accepted—various measures explicitly permitting or mandating discrimination against homosexuals. Other measures forbade state and local governments from including sexual orientation in the categories covered by antidiscrimination legislation.

Opponents of gay-rights measures drew support from a broad conservative backlash against what many Americans considered the excesses and immorality displayed by popular youth culture since the 1960s. Beginning in the 1970s and gaining widespread public support in the more conservative 1980s, campaigns against abortion, women's liberation, pornography, and homosexuality overlapped. These campaigns found supporters among the same pool of conservative Americans.

Prominent among these conservatives were evangelical Christians, who made up almost a quarter of the U.S. population. The various "anti-" campaigns drew increasing

THE MORAL MAJORITY

The Reverend Jerry Falwell *(left)*, a television evangelist, founded the group known as the Moral Majority in 1979. The organization brought together fundamentalist Christians into a formidable political force.

"WE WOULD NOT BE HAVING THE PRESENT MORAL CRISIS regarding the homosexual movement if men and women accepted their proper roles as designated by God. In the Christian home the father is responsible to exercise spiritual control and to be the head over his wife and children. . . . In the Christian home the woman is to be submissive. . . . Homosexuality is Satan's diabolical attack upon the family, God's order in Creation."

**—THE REVEREND JERRY FALWELL,
FOUNDER OF THE MORAL MAJORITY, 1980**

numbers of evangelicals into political activism. Many joined such religious-political organizations as the Reverend Jerry Falwell's Moral Majority (founded in 1979) and, later, the Christian Coalition (founded in 1989). This block of religious right voters and activists became increasingly important in U.S. politics. It came to dominate the Republican Party in the 1980s, 1990s, and into the twenty-first century. (As early as the 1984 election campaign, President Ronald Reagan voiced Republican solidarity with the religious right by vowing to "resist the efforts of some to obtain government endorsement of homosexuality.") The religious right has been the dominant voice against gay rights in the United States.

In 1981 a mysterious, deadly sickness afflicting gay men in the United States was first reported. News of the disease spread among gay men and lesbians in 1982 and among the general public in the mid-1980s. Scientists studying the disease called it acquired immunodeficiency syndrome (AIDS). The main symptom of AIDS was that a patient's natural immune system stopped functioning. AIDS patients thus suffered and died from infections that healthy people can easily fend off.

In the early years of the AIDS epidemic, its cause and mode of transmission were unknown. For a time, all that was generally known about AIDS was that it was deadly and that many homosexuals had it.

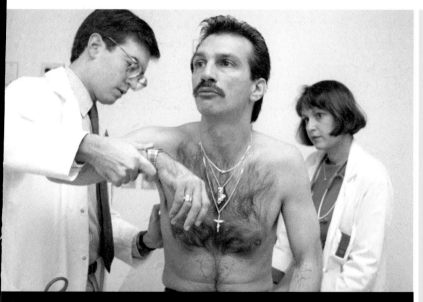

Doctors examine AIDS patient Russ Termini in 1989. Termini contracted AIDS in 1985. During the 1980s, large numbers of people in the United States were diagnosed with the disease, which is contracted through unprotected sex and sharing hypodermic needles.

This set off a wave of homophobia (fear and dislike of homo-sexuals) and antigay discrimination. Some medical personnel refused to treat AIDS patients. Some ambulance workers and police refused to touch patients who appeared to be gay. Some funeral homes refused to handle AIDS cases.

Eventually, scientists figured out that AIDS is caused by a virus, human immunodeficiency virus (HIV). HIV first infiltrated the male homosexual community in the United States sometime in the 1970s, where it quickly spread through sexual contact. HIV has since spread in the United States among heterosexuals and intravenous drug users, through sexual contact and the use of shared hypodermic needles.

The revelation in 1985 that actor Rock Hudson was ill with AIDS marked a turning point in public attitudes. By then people had a better understanding of the cause of the disease and of the ways it could and could not be transmitted. By then it was also known that AIDS wasn't just a "gay disease." Americans came to see AIDS as a disease like any other, requiring funding for research, treatment, and prevention—and compassion for its victims.

Because of the AIDS epidemic, gay men became the focus of more—often positive—media attention than ever before. In many ways, Americans demonstrated acceptance of homosexuals in public life and in the workplace. For example:

- In 1987 Congressman Barney Frank, a Democrat from Massachusetts, announced that he was gay. His con-stituents have returned him to Congress in every elec-tion since then.
- In 1991 a black lesbian, Sherry Harris, was elected mayor of Seattle.
- By the early 1990s, U.S. companies as diverse as the Lotus software company, Levi-Strauss, the *Boston Globe*,

Congressman Barney Frank of Massachusetts has been a member of the U.S. Congress since 1981. He publically announced that he was gay in 1987.

and the Apple computer company had granted spousal benefits, such as health insurance, to same-sex partners of their homosexual employees.

Also by the early 1990s, most of the largest of U.S. corporations had adopted formal nondiscrimination policies covering gay men and lesbians. (Most smaller companies, however, had no such formal policies.)

The AIDS epidemic drew unprecedented numbers of gay men out of the closet. It increased the visibility of the gay community. (By 1993 a majority of Americans polled said they knew at least one homosexual personally. That was up from just 25 to 30 percent in 1985.) The epidemic also diverted a lot of energy into the struggle to raise money for AIDS research and to prevent more infections. Much energy also went into the exhausting work of taking care of the sick and dying. Knowledge of the disease also made sex with many partners less attractive and committed, monogamous (single partner) relationships more attractive and admired among gay men. This fueled a growing demand for legal domestic partnership and marriage rights.

Thousands of homosexual couples struggling with horrible illness also had to deal with the consequences of having no legal family relationship with their partners. Often hospitals would not allow partners to visit or have a say in medical care. Undertakers would not allow them to specify funeral arrangements. Surviving partners sometimes found themselves locked out of their own homes or enmeshed in inheritance disputes and tax problems. Legal marriage would have automatically eliminated many of these problems. But the main focus of activists seeking to remedy the situation wasn't on making same-sex marriage legal. Instead, the focus was on more immediately practical measures. As a result, since the late 1980s, domestic partnership laws and policies have come to address some of these problems.

Meanwhile, growing numbers of same-sex couples, mostly lesbians, were bearing children with the intention of raising them as a two-parent, same-sex couple. As with gay couples coping with AIDS, same-sex partners raising children together face a host of problems. Once again, these problems resulted from having no legal family relationship to each other or to each other's children. These problems would not have existed if the couple had been legally married. Early on, homosexual families and their supporters tried to fix these problems, mainly through private contracts and public domestic partnership policy. In all cases, these were partial solutions at best.

In the 1990s, fewer homosexual men became infected with

Sue Hollenshead *(left);* her partner, Lori Collins *(right);* and their twin six-year-old daughters, Lexi and Allyson Collins, attend the White House Easter Egg Roll in Washington, D.C., on April 17, 2006. They are members of the Family Equality Council, a gay and lesbian parents' organization.

AIDS. Because of better medical treatments, the life spans for many Americans with AIDS lengthened. The gay-rights movement increasingly turned its attention once again to civil rights and public acceptance issues. As part of this new phase of activism, growing numbers of same-sex couples began to seek the right to marry.

CHAPTER TWO

Gay Marriage as a Religious Issue

Marriage in the United States has both a civil and a religious component. The civil component lies in the government's recognition and enforcement of a specific legal status for married people. When two people are officially married, they immediately and automatically become next of kin (person who is most closely related).

They are also legally linked in dozens of ways in which they weren't before their marriage. The religious component of marriage in the United States is separate from that of the government. Churches, synagogues, mosques, and other religious institutions may perform—or refuse to perform—religious marriage ceremonies for whomever they choose. Close to two-thirds of couples who've been legally married in the United States in recent years have chosen to have religious ceremonies. More than one-third have not.

Dale James Wallington *(left)* and state representative Art Feltman *(right)* participated in a civil union ceremony at city hall in Hartford, Connecticut, on October 1, 2005.

Although the United States is home to a kaleidoscope of religious faiths, it is predominantly Christian. Organized opposition to same-sex marriage has been overwhelmingly dominated by conservative, fundamentalist Christians. Their churches teach that the Bible is both literally true and is an instruction book for living properly. Most fundamentalists believe that homosexual behavior is sinful. Overall, those who believe that homosexuality is a sin typically also believe that it is a choice. They believe that homosexuality is a lifestyle you choose rather than a trait (such as race or eye color) you are born with. This point of view is contrary to what homosexuals themselves say. It is also contrary to current scientific understanding. Taking this line of reasoning a little further, however, it makes sense that those who believe that homosexuality is a personal but sinful choice will oppose any sort of social approval for it. They oppose legalizing same-sex marriage, lest that approval makes homosexuality more attractive and tempting. According to this line of thought, the social shame attached to homosexuality helps prevent children from being corrupted and helps weak people to avoid choosing to sin in that way.

On the other hand, religious people who believe that homosexuality is not sinful also tend to believe that it is an inherent characteristic. They believe that God created gay people gay and loves them as they are. Taking that line of reasoning a little further allows and encourages same-sex marriage as a way to enable homosexuals to live a kind of life that God is believed to approve. That kind of life—committed, one-partner relationships—avoids the sin of promiscuous sex outside marriage. In Christian scripture, the apostle Paul calls celibacy (abstinence from sexual intercourse) a "gift" from God. Paul is quite clear that this is not a gift God gives to everyone. For those who aren't so gifted, Paul advises marriage.

Interpretations of Jewish and Christian scripture regarding homosexuality have been as diverse as the personal histories, religious affiliations, and political agendas of the individuals who believe in them. Only a few Jewish or Christian scriptural references address or allude to homosexuality. None discusses it in the context of marriage. Those scriptures that do mention homosexuality are arguably not central to either faith. (Jesus never mentions homosexuality.) All the references are discussed in the next few paragraphs.

The Bible story most often cited concerning homosexuality is that of the city of Sodom. In Genesis 19, a man named Lot invited two strangers (angels in disguise) into his house in Sodom. After dinner "the men of Sodom, both young and old, all the people to the last man, surrounded the house; and they called to Lot, 'Where are the men who came to you tonight? Bring them out to us, that we may know them.'" Lot begged the Sodomites not to "act so wickedly," but they persisted. The angels struck the men blind. In the morning, God destroyed the entire city. (A similar story is told in Judges 19–20. In the New Testament of the Christian Bible, 2 Peter 2:6 and Jude 7 both refer to God's punishment of Sodom.)

Conservative American Christians have primarily interpreted this story as God punishing the Sodomites for homosexuality. They interpret the word *know* as meaning "to have sex with." Others, however, point out that the story makes more sense if the primary sin is inhospitality. Lot was not a native of Sodom, and his guests were likely suspected of spying. They say that the ancient word translated as "know" is ambiguous. For these reasons, they say that the Sodomites likely wanted to interrogate and perhaps execute Lot's guests. Even if homosexuality was involved, these revisionists argue, what they wanted to do was

Opponents of same-sex marriage rally at a demonstration in San Francisco, California, in 2004.

rape the strangers. And rape is immoral whether it's a man raping a man or a man raping a woman. ("Revisionist" scholars are those who put forth new interpretations of history or scripture.)

The revisionists have a harder time with Leviticus 18:22 ("You shall not lie with a male as with a woman; it is an abomination.") and Leviticus 20:13 ("If a man lies with a male as with a woman, both of them have committed an abomination; they shall be put to death, their blood is upon them.") The predominant Jewish and Christian interpretation of these passages is that homosexuality is a serious sin. Some revisionists argue, however, that the passages refer either specifically to male prostitutes associated with idol-worshipping cults or to ritual uncleanness rather than immoral behavior. ("Uncleanness" is a condition that also occurs if, for example, a man touches a corpse or a menstruating woman.)

In the New Testament, the apostle Paul in Romans 1:26–27 says: "For this reason God gave them [those who do not honor him] up to dishonorable passions. Their women exchanged natural relations for the unnatural, and the men likewise gave up natural relations with women and were consumed with passion for one another, men committing shameful acts with men and receiving in their own persons the due penalty for their error." Conservative Christians once again read this as a clear-cut condemnation of homosexuality. Revisionists note that Paul likely had in mind prostitutes and men who had sex with young boys. (Such relations, like rape, are immoral regardless of the sex of the individuals involved.) Another revisionist interpretation sees these verses as a description of presumably heterosexual people

Supporters of same-sex marriage gather outside the state house in Boston, Massachusetts, in January 2007. They oppose a constitutional amendment that would outlaw same-sex marriage.

(who had previously enjoyed heterosexual sex) acting against their God-given nature by having sex with same-sex partners. From this point of view, it would be just as sinful for homosexuals to reject their God-given homosexual nature by having sex with partners of the opposite sex.

Paul also apparently includes homosexuality in lists of sins in other passages. In 1 Corinthians 6:9–10, he says, "Do you know that the unrighteous will not inherit the kingdom of God? Do not be deceived; neither the immoral, nor idolaters, nor adulterers, nor homosexuals, nor thieves, nor the greedy, nor drunkards, nor revilers, nor robbers will inherit the kingdom of God." And in 1 Timothy 1:9–10, he says that "the law is not laid down for the just but for the lawless and sinners, for the unholy and profane, for murderers of fathers and murderers of mothers, for manslayers, immoral persons, sodomites, kidnapers, liars, perjurers." Revisionists, however, note that the true meaning of the ancient words translated here as "homosexuals" and "sodomites" is unclear. They might instead mean "prostitutes," "pederasts" (one who has anal intercourse with a boy), or "masturbators." Scripture can be and often has been cited in support of changing various rules for how people ought to live. This is especially true in Christian scripture, which presents a "new covenant" between God and humankind.

Religious beliefs and church policies toward same-sex marriage are currently unsettled in the United States. Religious organizations are divided on this issue, some bitterly. Same-sex marriages are being performed by some congregations and opposed by others in the same religious organization. Furthermore, many religious leaders who oppose religious marriage ceremonies for same-sex couples do support same-sex civil marriage or civil union. They view this position as a matter of justice or compassion. Many more refuse to support legal bans on same-sex marriage out of respect for separation of church and state. In their way of thinking, even if their churches find same-sex marriage, or sex outside of marriage, or anything else immoral, that isn't a good enough reason by itself to make it illegal. In short, American religious organizations are diverse, and so are their attitudes toward homosexuality.

Orthodox Judaism flatly forbids homosexuality. (So do Mormonism and Islam.) However, the Reform Judaism movement (which represents the largest number of American Jews) has endorsed civil rights protections for homosexuals. Some Reform congregations have been especially welcoming of gay men and lesbians. A few Reform rabbis have performed same-sex commitment ceremonies.

Since 1986 the Catholic Church has held that homosexual orientation is not in itself sinful but that all homosexual behavior is. Priests have been suspended from their duties and in some cases expelled from their orders for ministering to homosexuals. The Catholic Church opposes any legalization of same-sex marriage.

Some bishops of the Episcopal Church (the American branch of the Anglican Church) have ordained gay and lesbian priests and deacons. Some Episcopal priests have blessed same-sex unions. Anglican leadership outside the United States has been much less liberal about homosexuality.

Retiring Episcopal bishop Douglas Theuner *(right)* introduces the Reverend V. Gene Robinson *(left)* to church members in Concord, New Hampshire, in June 2003. New Hampshire Episcopalians elected Robinson, an openly gay man, to be their next bishop.

Among Protestants, the more liberal denominations have been more accommodating of homosexuality. Quakers and Unitarians, for example, have accepted and supported stable and committed gay relationships for decades. Middle-of-the-road Protestant denominations, such as Methodists, Lutherans, and Presbyterians, have generally opposed same-sex marriage. They have debated but not firmly concluded how to treat their gay parishioners.

Conservative Protestant denominations, most notably the Southern Baptists, have strongly condemned homosexuality as sinful. Since the 1970s, they have also spearheaded antigay-rights political activity in the United States. They oppose any legal recognition of same-sex marriage.

MACKY ALSTON AND HIS PARTNER WERE MARRIED in a large, church wedding ceremony. Despite the fact that the marriage was illegal in the state where they lived, the ceremony held great meaning for Macky and Nick. Macky expresses his feelings here:

"Our wedding was like an exorcism. It cast out our shame and replaced it with the recognition that we are loved by God and our community, and that our love is God-filled. We needed bells. We needed fanfare. We needed a cheering crowd. We needed a wedding. And that's what God delivered. . . . Something happened that day at the altar. Nick and I are not the same. . . . Our love was blessed then and there by God in a new way. We were wed."

—MACKY ALSTON, N.D.

Even among conservative and middle-of-the-road Christian denominations, many local churches and individual clergy have been more liberal and accepting toward homosexuals than their national governing bodies. For example, a local Baptist church in North Carolina attracted national attention in 1998. At that time, its members gave its ministers permission to bless "all loving, committed and exclusive relationships between two people"—including same-sex relationships.

Buddhism neither forbids nor condones homosexuality. Within these various religious traditions, gay men and lesbians have formed groups that provide fellowship. These groups also seek to reconcile homosexuality with their religious traditions. Some of these groups have been embraced by their churches' leadership. Some, such as the Catholic group Dignity, maintain an uneasy coexistence. And some have been "exiled" from their parent churches.

The Reverend Troy Perry founded Metropolitan Community Churches, a Christian ministry dedicated to serving gay men and lesbians.

In addition, some churches are specifically dedicated to ministering to gay men and lesbians. The best known of these are the Metropolitan Community Churches. This grew out of a Christian ministry founded by the Reverend Troy Perry in 1968. The organization includes hundreds of congregations worldwide and performs thousands of same-sex weddings each year.

RELIGION AND MARRIAGE

Some religious conservatives have focused less on what homosexuality is (a sin, in their view) and more on what it isn't—heterosexual marriage. They say that heterosexual marriage with children is God's model for how humans should live their lives. In their view, heterosexual marriage is the only context in which sex is holy. Scripture, they believe, provides a blueprint for how to live that married life. Homosexuality, they say, simply has no place in God's plan. In their view, same-sex marriage isn't marriage at all.

Religious homosexuals and other supporters of same-sex marriage, on the other hand, note that same-sex marriages can and, in many cases, do foster the same virtues that any godly marriage should. These virtues include love, commitment, raising children, taking care of family, and aiding the community.

Conservative religious opponents of same-sex marriage—mostly fundamentalist Christians—cite scripture not only in relation to homosexuality but also in relation to their view of heterosexual marriage. But marriage as described by scripture varies in many ways from what most people, religious people included, would approve. It would be hard, for example, to find many modern supporters of the Bible's approval of men having many wives and concubines. (Concubines in biblical times were women who belonged to a particular man, lived in his household, and had sex with him but were unmarried. King Solomon had seven hundred wives and three hundred concubines.) Nor would many modern people support the biblical requirement that if a married man dies, the man's brother must marry his widow.

Nonetheless, fundamentalist Christians assert that the Bible offers us in modern times a model for marriage that must not be tampered with. Marriage, according to their interpretation, is something created and blessed by God. Government can

OPINION MAKER

"We strongly oppose any legislative and judicial attempts, both at the state and federal levels, to grant same-sex unions the equivalent status and rights of marriage—by naming them marriage, civil unions, or by any other means."

—STATEMENT OF THE ADMINISTRATIVE COMMITTEE,
U.S. CONFERENCE OF CATHOLIC BISHOPS, 2003

acknowledge marriage, but it has no power to redefine it. "Natural" marriage, as this God-created institution is sometimes called by its proponents, is a union of one man and one woman. Within that union, the woman is to be submissive to the man. Although U.S. law on marriage in the past several decades has come to treat men and women pretty much the same, fundamentalist Christians have very different expectations for men and women in marriage. In their eyes, gay marriage is triply wrong. It validates homosexual behavior they consider sinful. It unites two men or two women instead of one of each as they believe God intended. And it validates marital roles that don't fit the biblical model of wives being submissive to husbands.

This is not the point of view of most religious people in the United States. Nor is that view any longer enforced by law for heterosexuals. Is it a simple injustice to continue to enforce the biblical model of marriage only for homosexuals? Or would legally recognizing same-sex marriage somehow damage the institution of marriage and do society more harm than good?

CHAPTER
THREE

What Kind of Country?

Religious arguments against same-sex marriage are reinforced by tradition. It's much more convincing to say "God says marriage is between one man and one woman" when it's been that way in our culture for centuries. But over time, the institution of marriage has changed. In recent decades, U.S. law and custom regarding marriage have changed a great deal. The debate about same-sex marriage is part of a wider debate about that process of change. The wider debate is about whether such change should continue, stop, or be rolled back.

CHANGES IN MARRIAGE RULES AND ROLES

Over past centuries, the United States—and Western civilization in general—has made a variety of changes to marriage law and custom. Many changes were controversial at the time. Still, most have come to be considered good by a vast majority of people. Among these changes is that married women are legally allowed to own and control their own property. Polygamy (a marriage in which one spouse may have more than one mate) has been made illegal. Dowries—payment by the bride or bride's family to the groom—are no longer expected. Parents may not choose spouses for their children without the child's consent. They may not veto their adult son's or daughter's choice of a spouse. People of different races may legally marry. Husbands are no longer legally entitled to rape their wives. And married couples have a legal right to obtain and use birth control.

Before the 1970s, laws concerning marriage generally applied differently to husbands and wives. From the early days of English common law, the wife's legal and economic identity was absorbed into her husband's upon marriage. (English common law was the foundation of the earliest U.S. laws on marriage.) The wife's property and future earnings became her husband's property. She could not own property or enter into contracts on her own. Her husband spoke (and voted) for her in all public matters. And her husband became legally responsible for providing economically for her and their children.

Change began, slowly, in the early nineteenth century. Between the 1830s and 1870s, most U.S. states passed laws

George Washington, the first president of the United States, married Mrs. Martha Dandridge Custis, a wealthy Virginia widow, on January 6, 1759. Through his marriage, Washington then gained control of the large Custis estate of his wife.

In September 1920, this woman handed over her ballot in the first election open to American women.

allowing women to continue to own property they had held before marriage or acquired during marriage. Ownership no longer automatically passed to the husband. Another wave of legal changes followed after women gained the right to vote in 1920. By the mid-1930s, married women in nearly every state could own property on their own. They could also sue in court and legally write their own wills. Since the 1970s, another wave of changes has moved the law further toward treating married men and women much the same. For example, modern-day courts and laws typically hold both husbands and wives responsible for providing economically for their spouses and children.

Another big change since the 1970s has been in divorce. Divorce used to be so difficult—and so disgraceful—that in 1870 the divorce rate was fewer than two in one thousand marriages. In 1900 it had risen to only four in one thousand. To obtain a divorce, a person had to prove that his or her spouse was at fault

41

in one or more ways specified by law. Adultery and desertion were the usual reasons. But in many states, extreme cruelty or habitual drunkenness would do. In 1969 California became the first state to adopt a "no-fault" divorce law. The new law allowed a couple to get a divorce if both spouses agreed to it. Neither spouse had to prove the other at fault for anything. Within four years, more than two-thirds of the other states had adopted some form of no-fault divorce. By 1985 every state had done so. Since then the divorce rate has soared. About half of all marriages end in divorce.

Along with these changes in marriage law, many other changes have evolved in the range of living and family arrangements that are considered normal. In recent decades, the number of adults living alone and unmarried has increased. In the late 1990s, about half of all U.S. adults were married. That was down from three-quarters in the early 1970s. The number of unmarried couples living together increased almost ten times between 1960 and the late 1990s. That was five times as fast as the increase in the total number of U.S. households. On average, people are getting married at an older age. Typically, they live alone or with friends or prospective spouses before marriage.

NO-FAULT DIVORCE

THE IDEA BEHIND THE FAMILY Research Council (FRC) began at the 1980 White House Conference on Families. The organization promotes marriage and family as the foundation of civilization. The FRC seeks to influence public debate and public policy concerning abortion, the institution of marriage, and family life. Tony Perkins became president of the FRC in 2003. Here is what he has said about no-fault divorce:

"No-fault divorce was a public policy initiative that has knocked the institution of marriage to its knees and weakened it to the point that homosexual radicals are now moving in for the kill."

—TONY PERKINS, PRESIDENT OF FAMILY RESEARCH COUNCIL, 2004

Decades ago it was more typical to move directly from their parents' home to their marital home. It has become the norm for heterosexual couples to live together before marriage. Promiscuity (casual sex with more than one partner) and sex without love still carry a stigma for most Americans. But premarital sex between loving but unmarried partners is generally accepted by society.

The number of unmarried mothers giving birth has increased dramatically. The number of children living with only one parent has also increased. People living in "traditional" family circumstances—breadwinner dad and stay-at-home mom raising kids—have since the 1970s become a tiny minority. By 1999 only about one-quarter of U.S. adults were married and living with children. Many of the moms in those households were working full-time outside the home. Women, including a majority of women with children under six years of age, make up almost half of the U.S. workforce.

Dorothy Petersen of Carterville, Illinois, is a single mother of four. Inadequate income is a frequent problem for single parents. To compensate, they often have to take on additional jobs in order to meet their monthly expenses.

Underlying all these changes is a shift away from the belief that sex roles, within or outside marriage, are unchanging and universal, let alone something the government should enforce. Most people living in the United States believe that men and women should be free to express and pursue their talents and preferences as best they can. Most people think this should be so whether or not the results match traditional, sex-specific expectations for men and women.

Religious conservatives opposing same-sex marriage have opposed virtually all of these trends. The have opposed equal legal status for wives and husbands. They have also opposed easier divorces, premarital sex, the blurring of boundaries between the sexes, and women working outside the home. Their claim is that these changes undermine the order God has decreed for society. That order, they believe, is based on a family in which a breadwinner husband takes care of a stay-at-home wife and children, who submit to his authority.

PURPOSES OF MARRIAGE

FOCUS ON THE FAMILY IS A CHRISTIAN ORGANIZATION that concerns itself with issues related to the family. Its view of marriage as expressed in the quotes below stems from those roots. Here's what two writers affiliated with Focus on the Family say about the purposes of marriage:

"God has weaved marriage into human nature so that it serves two primary purposes throughout all societies:

"Marriage always brings male and female adults together into committed sexual relationships in order to regulate sexuality and provide for the needs of daily life. Wives help men channel their sexual energy in socially productive and nonpredatory ways. Husbands help protect women from the exploitation of other males.

"Marriage ensures that children have the benefits of both their mother and their father, each in their distinctive and unique ways."

—GLENN T. STANTON AND BILL MAIER, 2004

The cast of the popular television show *Will and Grace* are shown here in 2001 after receiving awards for Outstanding Performance by an Ensemble Cast in a Comedy Series at the Screen Actors Guild Awards. *Will and Grace*, which had gay characters and a theme centered on homosexuality, ran from 1998 until 2006.

SAME-SEX MARRIAGE AS A CIVIL RIGHTS ISSUE

Religious conservatives have also opposed the trend in the United States toward greater public acceptance of homosexuals. As recently as the 1960s and 1970s, most people considered it socially acceptable to casually ridicule homosexuals and homosexuality. By the 1990s, homosexual characters were being portrayed sympathetically on TV and in mainstream movies. Substantial numbers of respected public figures—politicians, performers, and businesspeople—had begun to openly acknowledge their own homosexuality. Public opinion had shifted toward a live-and-let-live attitude. Even many religious conservatives, who continue to see homosexual behavior as sinful, support a range of civil rights for homosexuals, such as a right to equal employment opportunities. In 1977 only 56 percent of Americans believed that homosexuals should have equal employment rights. By 2004, 89 percent supported this idea.

Advocates for same-sex marriage sometimes cite the 1967

U.S. Supreme Court decision, *Loving v. Virginia*. That decision struck down state laws banning interracial marriage. They note that a majority of the U.S. public opposed interracial marriage at that time. But times have changed. Almost everyone has come to agree that the law should allow people of different races to marry.

A BASIC CIVIL RIGHT

Richard P. Loving *(right)* and his wife, Mildred *(left),* married in Washington, D.C., in 1958. When they returned home to Virginia, they were convicted under a Virginia law that banned interracial unions. Not until 1967 did the U.S. Supreme Court overturn that law in the *Loving v. Virginia* case.

"THE FREEDOM TO MARRY HAS LONG BEEN RECOGNIZED as one of the vital personal rights essential to the orderly pursuit of happiness by free men.

"Marriage is one of the 'basic civil rights of man,' fundamental to our very existence and survival. . . . The Fourteenth Amendment requires that the freedom of choice to marry not be restricted by invidious racial discriminations. Under our Constitution, the freedom to marry, or not marry, a person of another race resides with the individual and cannot be infringed by the State."

—CHIEF JUSTICE EARL WARREN, WRITING THE MAJORITY OPINION FOR THE U.S. SUPREME COURT IN *LOVING V. VIRGINIA*, 1967

Those who see same-sex marriage as a civil rights issue typically present it as a similar matter of equal justice under the law. Some draw a sharp line between public and private discrimination. According to this way of thinking, the state should be required to issue marriage licenses to two men or two women under the same rules it uses for heterosexual couples. But at the same time, private institutions such as churches would still be free to refuse to marry same-sex couples.

OPPOSITION TO SAME-SEX MARRIAGE

Most of the U.S. opposition to legalizing same-sex marriage comes from conservative Christians. Their arguments against same-sex marriage are mostly but not completely religious in nature.

Two of the weaker arguments against same-sex marriage focus on procreation and polygamy. The basis of the procreation argument is that society offers privileges to married couples because marriage can result in the birth and care of children. According to this argument, same-sex marriage isn't valid because two men or two women can't, by themselves, make babies. This argument is weakened by the fact that society doesn't expect male-female couples be able to bear children as a requirement of being married. Heterosexuals who are sterile, or who are unwilling or too old to have children are not forbidden to marry. Indeed, the law explicitly recognizes the right of married couples not to have children. (In 1965 in *Griswold v. Connecticut*, the U.S. Supreme Court cited a right to marital privacy in striking down a state law banning access to birth-control devices.) In addition, many homosexuals who want to marry already have children, intend to have them, or wish to adopt them.

The polygamy argument is a variation on the "slippery slope" idea. It is based on the notion that once you start down a slippery slope, it's hard to stop. If you extend the definition of marriage beyond one man and one woman to include same-sex couples, the argument goes, you're on the road to "anything goes," including polygamy. This argument is strong only if you accept that marriage is a natural (not established by humans) phenomenon created by God. Those who believe in "natural" marriage believe it is something humans should not tamper with. They do not see marriage as an institution established by humans and therefore changeable as other legal and social arrangements are. They worry that "if marriage breaks free and overflows its natural boundaries, conforming only to the personal preferences of individuals, then it will lose any definite shape and flood out of control," as a pair of writers affiliated with Focus on the Family have put it. But, on the other hand, if marriage (or at least government recognition and regulation of marriage) is essentially a human

Tom Green *(top center in dark suit)* of Utah is pictured here with his five wives and twenty-five children. Opponents of same-sex marriage argue that extending the definition of marriage to include homosexual couples could lead to making polygamous marriage legal across the United States.

institution, there's no logical or constitutional reason why society can't legalize same-sex marriage without going further. Marriage could still be reserved for any two people willing to make a lifetime commitment to each other.

Other arguments against same-sex marriage are subtler and more difficult to refute. For example, some opponents of same-sex marriage say that calling it "marriage" is telling a lie. From that, they say, it follows that government recognition of such marriages endorses that lie and conveys the socially harmful message that, for the government, truth doesn't matter. According to Robert H. Knight of the Family Research Council, "to describe such [homosexual] relationships as 'marriage' destroys the definition of marriage altogether. . . . Destroying definitions does enormous damage not only to marriage but to the idea of truth. Calling two lesbians a 'marriage' is telling a lie, and official recognition of this breeds the sort of cynicism found in totalitarian countries, where lies are common currency."

OPINION MAKER

"Societies must have intact families to survive; societies do not need any homosexual relationships in order to flourish. To equate them [heterosexual and homosexual relationships] is to lie about them."

—ROBERT H. KNIGHT OF THE FAMILY RESEARCH COUNCIL, 1994

Another argument made by opponents of same-sex marriage is that gay-rights activists have primarily pursued legalized same-sex marriage in an undemocratic way. They've tried to change the law through court challenges rather than through state legislatures or voter referenda (having citizens vote on the issue). Opponents decry this use of the courts as "judicial activism."

From their viewpoint, opponents say that gay-rights activists are asking judges to arrogantly force a minority viewpoint on the majority. However, supporters say that this is a normal part of the way democracy works in the United States. They point out that one of the functions of the courts is to protect minority rights. They refer to the history of the racial civil rights movement. This history, they say, tells us that when courts make just decisions that are controversial at the time, the majority will eventually see the justice in them.

The primary arguments against same-sex marriage, though, relate to the fundamentalist religious idea that God has decreed that marriage is a union between one man and one woman. Those who believe this are opposed to same-sex marriage. Like easier divorce and all the other recent changes in marriage customs and

The U.S. Supreme Court justices, photographed here in 2006, are *(first row from left)* Anthony Kennedy, John Paul Stevens, John Roberts, Antonin Scalia, David Souter, *(second row from left)* Stephen Breyer, Clarence Thomas, Ruth Bader Ginsburg, and Samuel Alito. Most of the movement to legalize same-sex marriage is happening in lower courts, one case at a time, and in state legislatures.

family life, it "promotes a smorgasbord mentality for family life: choose what suits your tastes, and one choice is as good as another," as authors Glenn Stanton and Bill Maier put it.

For conservative fundamentalists, one choice is not as good as another. They beleive that virtuous choices by individuals contribute to a strong, healthy society. Making and sticking with virtuous choices is often difficult. So society encourages such choices in many ways. Conservative fundamentalists, such as those affiliated with Focus on the Family, believe that extending those benefits to same-sex couples would imply that society condones and encourages same-sex marriage. They believe that this practice would only worsen an already bad set of trends in family life and in society as a whole. Stanton and Maier write, "The decline of marriage over the past few decades has reduced the number of men who are helping women raise their children, creating widespread fatherlessness, one of our nation's most urgent social problems. Same-sex marriage likely will contribute to this decline, even among heterosexual men. Won't lesbian families send the message to men that fathers are optional and lead men to increasingly see themselves that way? Gay male families tell us that a man committing himself to one woman is simply one lifestyle choice among many. So, men committing themselves to

Religious conservatives believe that the God-given model for the family is a married man and woman and their children.

women will become increasingly optional. This is not good for men, and it won't be good for women or their children."

More broadly, same-sex marriage is opposed by many religious conservatives on the grounds that it denies and subverts God-given differences between men and women. Traditional marriage, they believe, benefits husband and wife, their children, and society as a whole. It does this because it brings men and women together in a cooperative, committed, loving relationship while maintaining their differences. According to this way of thinking, same-sex marriage is damaging to society because it implies that the only absolute difference between men and women is biological, in their reproductive organs. This line of thought implies that beyond the production of sperm or eggs, individuals and couples are free to define their roles as they wish. Opponents of same-sex marriage see this as a denial of and insult to our humanity. According to Stanton and Maier, "Granting moral equality to even one same-sex marriage diminishes all of us at the very core of our humanity. . . . Same-sex families—when not just merely tolerated but seen as socially equal to natural marriage and families—announce that the only inherent virtues male and female hold for the family are in their genetic, biological contributions to procreation: sperm, egg and womb. It is dehumanizing to reduce male and female to these impersonal dimensions because in deep and profound ways personhood, marriage and family is beautifully and intrinsically tied to gender. As we lose this, we lose an essential part of our humanity."

DIFFERENT OPINIONS AMONG GAY ACTIVISTS

Most homosexuals in the United States see same-sex marriage as a civil rights issue. They say that government recognition of marriage is a very basic public institution should be available to same-sex couples in the same way that it's available to heterosexual couples. Some gay and lesbian activists, however, have

A NEW POLITICS

IN HIS 1995 BOOK *VIRTUALLY NORMAL*, the conservative gay writer Andrew Sullivan suggests a "politics of homosexuality" that "affirms a simple and limited principle: that all public (as opposed to private) discrimination against homosexuals [should] be ended and that every right and responsibility that heterosexuals enjoy as public citizens be extended [to homosexuals].

"The centerpiece of this new politics . . . of public equality-private freedom . . . is equal access to civil marriage. . . . Marriage is not simply a private contract; it is a social and public recognition of a private commitment. As such, it is the highest public recognition of personal integrity. Denying it to homosexuals is the most public affront possible to their public equality. . . .

"If nothing else were done at all, and gay marriage were legalized, 90 percent of the political work necessary to achieve gay and lesbian equality would have been achieved. It is ultimately the only reform that truly matters."

—Andrew Sullivan, 1995

opposed including marriage on the gay-rights agenda. Their concern is that making marriage available to homosexuals will tend to pressure same-sex couples into oppressive and inappropriate marital roles derived from marriage's history of men exercising authority over women. A related concern is that monogamous marriage would become so much the norm, so generally expected, that it would further stigmatize homosexuals who don't choose to settle down with one partner.

Other activists say that is exactly the point. If homosexuals are truly accepted into the U.S. mainstream, they'll be held to the same values as heterosexuals. One of those values is that married monogamy is given greater respect and support than sexual promiscuity. Marriage, according to this way of thinking, must be made available to same-sex couples as part of their full acceptance as equal citizens in U.S. society.

Still others respond that legalizing same-sex marriage would create opportunities to radically transform the way everyone—heterosexuals as well as homosexuals—sees marriage. Legalizing same-sex marriage could make marriage more egalitarian and less patriarchal (male dominated). It might become more difficult to use marriage as a tool of male oppression of females. Certainly, thinking of two men as husband and husband or two women as wife and wife shakes up our thinking about the range of possibilities for the roles of "husband" and "wife." (And that's precisely what the strongest opponents of same-sex marriage say is most wrong with it.)

THE CONSERVATIVE CASE FOR SAME-SEX MARRIAGE

A very good conservative case can be made for legalizing same-sex marriage. Conservatives of all sorts—religious and nonreligious alike—typically agree that sexual promiscuity is wrong. As the Family Research Council's Robert H. Knight puts it, "If a culture does not discourage extramarital sexuality, the stable marriages are threatened because of the erosion of cultural, social, and, finally, legal support." Sexual promiscuity, to this way of thinking, is risky, unhealthy behavior. Such behavior is bad for society as well as for the individuals directly involved. Making marriage available to and rewarding for heterosexuals discourages promiscuity and encourages monogamy. It encourages commitment and other virtues that are good for both the individuals who

A COMMITMENT CEREMONY

BARBARA J. COX DESCRIBES HER FEELINGS AND EXPERIENCES related to her commitment ceremony:

"When my partner and I decided to have a commitment ceremony, we did so to express the love and caring that we feel for one another, to celebrate that love with our friends and family, and to express that love openly and with pride. . . . Some of the most politically 'out' experience I have ever had happened during those months of preparing for and having that ceremony. . . . Is it not profoundly transformative to speak so openly about lesbian love and commitment? The impact was so wide-ranging, not just on my partner and myself, but on our families, our friends, even the clerks in the jewelry stores when we explained we were looking for wedding rings for both of us."

—BARBARA J. COX, 1994

Jon Galluccino *(left)* and Michael Galluccino *(right)* exchange wedding vows on June 21, 1998, at the Episcopal Church of the Atonement in Fair Lawn, New Jersey.

practice them and for society overall. Barring marriage to homosexuals discourages all those good things. It encourages promiscuity and all the evils that come with it, some say. For these reasons, many conservatives (at least those conservatives who don't believe homosexuality itself is evil) should be advocates for same-sex marriage instead of opposing it.

Of course people can and often do choose to be virtuous without society rewarding them for it. Many unmarried homosexual couples are as committed and true to each other as any married, heterosexual couple. Preventing such committed couples from marrying arguably weakens the institution of marriage. As society becomes more accepting of homosexuality and openly homosexual couples become valued members of their communities, the distinction between marriage and living together without marriage blurs. The distinction seems less and less important to more and more people. As the social benefits of marriage become available to these unmarried couples, marriage becomes a less good deal. If, in addition, many or all the legal and practical benefits of marriage become available to unmarried couples through domestic partnership arrangements, the risk is that marriage will become largely irrelevant.

CHAPTER FOUR

Domestic Partnership

Marriage is in part a contract between two people and the society in which they live. In return for promising to take care of each other, society grants married people a wide array of benefits and tools. These encourage and enable them to do that well. Legal marriage grants all of these tools and benefits automatically. Domestic partnership arrangements address only some selected benefits.

Doug Braun *(right)* and Brian DeWitt *(left)* have been partners for fourteen years. They added their names to a domestic partner registry in Cleveland Heights, Ohio, on January 24, 2004.

RIGHTS, BENEFITS, AND OBLIGATIONS OF MARRIAGE

Marriage automatically makes couples next of kin. This carries with it a host of legal rights and obligations that make family life easier. Federal law specifies more than one thousand ways in which the U.S. government treats married people as a distinct class. Each of those thousand distinctions confers a special status, right, or benefit. (Most of these distinctions are connected with Social Security, veterans' benefits, and federal income, estate, and gift taxes.) State laws

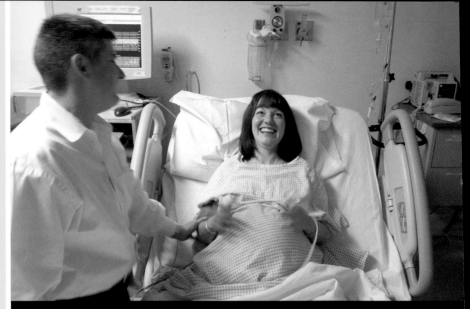

Partners Lori *(left)* and Wendy *(right)* share a moment of anticipation before the birth of their son Joshua at the John Muir Medical Center in Walnut Creek, California. Because they are not legally married, Lori could be denied the right to visit Wendy in the hospital.

create their own provisions, which vary from state to state. Typically, such provisions include the right to visit one's spouse in the hospital and to participate in medical decisions, to visit a spouse in jail, to make funeral arrangements for a spouse, and to co-own a spouse's property. They also typically include parental and inheritance rights. Employers and private institutions also grant benefits to married people. These range from health insurance for family members to membership benefits at museums, the YMCA, public swimming pools, and private golf courses.

Unmarried same-sex partners aren't considered "family," by law or by custom. This makes the routine comfort and care unmarried family members give one another when they're in need more difficult. Employers can refuse to give an employee family leave time to care for a same-sex partner or that partner's children. Hospitals can refuse to allow same-sex partners to visit or participate in the care of loved ones. Insurers generally refuse to allow unmarried couples to have a policy covering the whole family. Partners with good retirement or health benefits most often can't share them with their same-sex mates. Married couples can. Nor can a same-sex partner collect unemployment benefits when quitting a job to follow his or her partner to a new job in a distant place. Legally married spouses can. An unmarried homosexual partner can't claim legal residence status for his or her partner when that partner is not a U.S. citizen. Heterosexual partners can gain legal residence status through marriage.

Same-sex couples can make arrangements with lawyers that partly simulate the legal relationship of married couples—but only partly. They can designate each other as beneficiaries in wills. They can authorize each other to make medical decisions in case of illness. In some states, they can adopt each other's children. But no lawyer can compel an employer to recognize an unmarried employee's partner as a spouse eligible for health insurance and other benefits. No lawyer can arrange spousal Social Security benefits for same-sex partners. No lawyer can enable same-sex couples to file joint tax returns—or to claim any of the many benefits the U.S. government gives married couples.

OPINION MAKER

"Marriage uniquely permits couples to travel and deal with others in business or across borders without playing a game of 'now you're legally next of kin; now you're legally not.'"

—SAME-SEX MARRIAGE ACTIVIST EVAN WOLFSON, 2004

DOMESTIC PARTNERSHIP ARRANGEMENTS BY GOVERNMENT AND EMPLOYERS

A surprising number of major employers have made benefits originally granted to employees' spouses available to their homosexual employees' partners. This is in part perhaps a reflection of the multinational nature of most large corporations. In other countries in which they do business (including those in most of Western Europe), domestic partnership status that is legally equivalent or close to marriage is available to same-sex couples. However, it's also obvious that these companies have decided that making such benefits available is good for their business. For major U.S. employers, granting benefits to same-sex partners of employees is a relatively recent development. The practice developed as public acceptance of homosexuality increased. In 1992 the software company Lotus became the first U.S. company with publicly traded stock (a company controlled by its stockholders rather than being privately owned) to offer such benefits. By the end of that year, twelve of the top five hundred companies in the United States offered benefits such as health insurance to their employees' same-sex partners. By 2004 more than two hundred did so.

Lotus is one U.S. company that offers benefits to the same-sex partners of its employees.

Meanwhile, dozens of local governments (beginning in 1984 with Berkeley, California) have granted same-sex partners of their employees the same benefits granted to legal spouses. Some state governments have granted such benefits too. In 1994 Vermont became the first state to grant health insurance benefits to same-sex partners of state employees.

Other state and local governments have set up official domestic partner registries. These are available to unmarried heterosexuals and homosexuals alike. By signing up with such a registry, partners become qualified for whatever domestic partnership benefits government or private institutions decide to grant them. California first set up a registry in 1999. At that time, state law specified only a few benefits associated with the registry. One benefit was the right to visit a partner in the hospital as next of kin. In September 2003, California's governor signed a bill assigning a long list of benefits and responsibilities to domestic partners. This bill made registering for domestic partnership similar to getting married in terms of its legal effects within the state. The states of Hawaii, New Jersey, and Maine, as well as several dozen local and county municipalities, have established domestic partnership registries with more limited effects. The U.S. government offers no such registry or benefits for unmarried partners.

DIFFERENT POINTS OF VIEW ON DOMESTIC PARTNERSHIP

Most support for legal status or employee benefits for domestic partners comes from people who believe it's only decent and fair. To them it seems unfair not to extend some of the benefits previously reserved for married people to committed couples who are ineligible to marry only because they're homosexual. Most who support this view assume that same-sex marriage is unlikely to become fully legal anytime soon. Many see domestic partnership as either better than nothing or as a reasonable compromise with people who oppose same-sex marriage.

THE TUCSON DOMESTIC PARTNERSHIP (DP) ORDINANCE

THE CITY OF TUSCON, ARIZONA, ENACTED A LAW, effective since December 1, 2003, that established a voluntary registry for domestic partners. Below is a description of the city's domestic partnership law as is written in the ordinance.

The Tucson Domestic Partnership (DP) Ordinance is a city law that provides a registry for domestic partners who wish to register. This is a means by which unmarried couples who share a relationship of mutual support, caring and commitment may document their relationship. This is the first domestic partner registry law in the state of Arizona.

Domestic partners are two people who sign a statement affirming that they:

• are not related by blood closer than would bar marriage in the State of Arizona;
• are not married to another person in a marriage expressly recognized by the State of Arizona or in any domestic partnership and/or civil union with another person;
• are both 18 years of age or older;
• are both competent to enter into a contract;
• both declare that they are each other's sole domestic partner;
• both currently share a primary residence, are in a relationship of mutual support, and declare that they intend to remain in such for the indefinite future. . . .

The ordinance lists two rights or benefits for registered partners in the City of Tucson: (1) a right to visitation of one's partner in a health care facility, as long as the patient consents; and (2) extending use of and access to city facilities to a registered domestic partner as if the domestic partner were a spouse.

Because Tucson's Domestic Partnership Ordinance is a city law, it cannot address or create rights, privileges, or responsibilities that might be available to spouses or partners under state or federal law.

Partners should consult an attorney and/or make arrangements for a number of important matters, including but not limited to:

• wills
• medical matters
• finances and powers of attorney
• children and dependents
• medical and health care employment benefits

But some people—on both sides of the debate—see domestic partnership as a radical way of reordering society. On the side supporting domestic partnership, some see the institution of marriage as sexist, conformist, repressive, and outmoded. They believe that it's wrong for society to favor the institution of marriage and would like to see the legal benefits of marriage distributed to a wide range of different kinds of relationships. Those relationships might include gay relationships, straight couples, just friends, and maybe even groups of friends.

On the other side, activists opposed to domestic partnership benefits for same-sex couples view such goals with alarm. "For several years," the Family Research Council's Robert H. Knight wrote in 1994, "homosexual activists have promoted the extension of marital benefits to same-sex couples (and, in some cases, unmarried heterosexual couples) in corporations and in the law. This practice, called 'domestic partnerships,' is billed as an extension of tolerance and civil rights, but would actually undermine the institutions of marriage and family. . . . Some jurisdictions are moving toward redefining the family to include same-sex relationships, and there is a movement within the legal community to overhaul the definitions of marriage and family. . . . The whole point is to demote marriage to a level with all other conceivable relationships."

Knight's argument is strengthened by the fact that domestic partnership isn't just for same-sex couples. In recent years, millions of heterosexual couples have chosen to live together without marriage. (The U.S. Census tells us that between 1990 and 2000, households with unmarried partners living together increased by 72 percent. By 2000 there were more than 5 million such couples. By far most of these couples were heterosexual.) Many domestic partnership arrangements are available to these couples too. The idea of granting benefits and privileges previously reserved for married people to couples who are able to marry but are unwilling to make that commitment makes many people uneasy. The concern here is that the institution of marriage will be weakened by making available "marriage lite" options such as domestic partnership. To this way of thinking, society should not offer the benefits of marriage without demanding that couples accept its responsibilities and obligations as well.

Domestic partnership describes a businesslike arrangement. It might consist of a contractual sharing of household responsibility, finances, or other legalities. Marriage includes this sort of contractual relationship, but that's not at its core. Marriage, for most people, is primarily about love, intimacy, and shared lives until death do us part. That domestic partnership doesn't necessarily involve these expectations may be both its strength and its

City clerk Mary Jean Sell *(left)* of Eureka Springs, Arkansas, hands Marie Howard *(right)* a certificate that recognizes the domestic partnership that Howard and her partner, Trella Laughlin *(center)*, have shared for thirty-nine years.

HERE ARE A FEW VIEWS ON MARRIAGE from those who favor same-sex unions and domestic partnership:

"To whatever extent they mimic marriage, domestic-partner programs send the message that, from the law's and thus society's point of view, marriage is no longer unique. On the other hand, to whatever extent they fall short of marriage, domestic-partner programs fail to give same-sex couples what they need."

—SAME-SEX MARRIAGE ADVOCATE JONATHAN RAUCH, 2004

"In Europe and North America, the flood that threatens the house of marriage is not gay marriage but heterosexual nonmarriage, including cohabitation, domestic partnerships, and other 'marriage lite' alternatives to marriage, all of which promise to offer the benefits of partnership without the burdens of marriage."

**—DAVID G. MYERS AND LETHA DAWSON SCANZONI,
CHRISTIAN WRITERS FAVORING LEGALIZATION OF SAME-SEX MARRIAGE, 2005**

"The lesbian and gay community has laid the groundwork for revolutionizing society's views of the family. The domestic partnership movement has been an important part of this progress insofar as it validates nonmarital relationships. Because it is not limited to sexual or romantic relationships, domestic partnership provides an important opportunity for many who are not related by blood or marriage to claim certain minimal protections. It is crucial, though, that we avoid the pitfall of framing the push for legal recognition of domestic partners (those who share a primary residence and financial responsibilities for each other) as a stepping-stone to marriage. We must keep our eyes on the goals of providing true alternatives to marriage and of radically reordering society's view of family."

—LAWYER AND LESBIAN ACTIVIST PAULA L. ETTELBRICK, 1989

DOMESTIC PARTNERSHIP

weakness. It's a strength in that people uncomfortable with same-sex marriage may be more willing to accept domestic partnership arrangements that don't claim to be marriage. It's a weakness in that domestic partnership offers same-sex couples only half a loaf. It offers a "marriage" that lacks the very expectations that are central to marriage for most people.

Marriage has a history. It has legal and social meaning. For many people, it has religious meaning as well. Society does not allow same-sex couples in domestic partnerships to claim those values for themselves. Conservative religious opponents of same-sex marriage

OPINION MAKER

"One of the main protections that comes with marriage is the word marriage, which brings clarity and security that is simply not replaceable by any other word or by a sheaf of documents."

—EVAN WOLFSON, 2004

believe that's a good thing. Most advocates of same-sex marriage strongly disagree.

To some observers, domestic partnerships look like a cover for bigotry. Legal scholar Evan Gerstmann writes that "if the government told Jews or Muslims or Hindus that they could have all the legal protections and religious freedoms enjoyed by Christians as long as they did not hold themselves out as 'religions,' the stigma inherent in such an offer would be obvious." Even domestic partnerships offering all the legal protections of marriage but not allowing the partners to call themselves married would carry such a stigma.

CHAPTER
FIVE

Gay Family Life

In 2000 the U.S. Census Bureau counted about 600,000 same-sex couples sharing households. Children were living in 28 percent of these households. This was probably an undercount. But even so, it means that probably more than 200,000 children—and maybe well over 300,000—are living with two homosexual parents or a parent and partner. In addition, gay family life includes countless homosexual children who live with their heterosexual parents.

Gay men and lesbians have often had children in heterosexual marriages before acknowledging their homosexuality. Many of these children have then been raised in part or entirely by one parent and a same-sex partner. (Some opponents of same-sex marriage point to prior heterosexual behavior as evidence that homosexuality is a lifestyle choice rather than an unchangeable condition. Homosexuals themselves, though,

In February 2004, Alex D'Amario *(left)* and Margot McShane *(right)* of Napa Valley, California, became the fourth same-sex couple to receive a marriage license in San Francisco. D'Amario is four months pregnant with twins in this photo.

71

Bill Dunn *(left)* holds five-year-old Hayden while Shaun Morse holds two-year-old Henry and six-year-old Nathan on the porch of their Wichita, Kansas, home. Both men are listed as parents of the couple's adopted children.

counter that such heterosexual relationships typically come from social pressure and a desire for family in a culture that discourages gay family life.) In addition, lesbians have long used artificial insemination (the introduction of semen into the uterus by other than natural means) to become pregnant. In some cases, mixed groups of gay men and lesbians have collaborated on conceiving and raising children. In recent years, a small number of gay men have hired women to become pregnant through artificial insemination and to bear their children. That arrangement lets gay men raise children to whom they are biologically related.

Antihomosexual activists considered all of these arrangements an outrage. They believe that children need heterosexual parents as role models. Still, the religious right strongly supports parents' rights to raise their children as they see fit. They have rarely sought to restrict the parental rights of homosexual biological parents.

CUSTODY AND ADOPTION

Antihomosexual activists have not been so restrained about custody disputes and adoption. In those cases, they have encouraged courts to consider homosexuality a strong negative trait. In courts that take that approach, a gay or lesbian parent has to overcome that black mark to win custody or visitation rights to children. Antihomosexual activists have also encouraged outright bans on adoption by homosexuals.

As of 2006, several states restricted adoptions by homosexuals:

- Florida law specifically bans adoption by homosexuals.
- Mississippi bans adoption by "same-sex couples."
- A directive from the state agency responsible for adoption in Nebraska bans adoption by known homosexuals and unmarried couples.
- Oklahoma refuses to recognize joint or second-parent adoptions previously made by same-sex couples who move to Oklahoma from another state.

Della Nagle *(second from left)* and Ruth Pinkham *(second from right)* of San Antonio, Texas, are raising five children together. Two are Della's biological children, one is adopted, and two are foster children.

- Utah bans adoption by cohabiting unmarried couples, regardless of whether they're the same-sex or heterosexual.

In addition, most other states have made it difficult for anyone other than married heterosexuals to adopt a child. Many states, for example, have required two separate adoption proceedings (one for each same-sex partner). That is a lengthy and expensive process.

The adoption issue most relevant to most same-sex couples with children is "second-parent" adoption. This is automatic for married heterosexuals. If the wife has a child through artificial insemination, her husband automatically becomes the child's legal father. Not so for lesbian couples. For them, the partner who didn't give birth has to go through an expensive and intrusive legal adoption process. And the state they live in may not even allow such adoptions. As of 2004, second-parent adoptions with two mothers or two fathers were allowed in nine states (California, Connecticut, Illinois, Indiana, Massachusetts, Pennsylvania, New York, New Jersey, and Vermont) and the District of Columbia. Such adoptions were also allowed in some counties in at least fifteen other states. Such adoptions were denied in Colorado, Ohio, and Wisconsin and in states that generally restrict adoption by homosexuals.

However, both public attitudes and court biases about adoption by homosexuals have been changing. In 1977 only 14 percent

OPINION MAKER

"The two-parent family—a man and a woman united in marriage—is the best environment in which to raise children. Public policy should uphold the two-parent family."

—FAMILY RESEARCH COUNCIL, N.D.

of those polled in the United States said that homosexuals should be allowed to adopt children. In 1992 that number had increased to 29 percent. By 2000 the figure had risen to 50 percent. Meanwhile, state and local courts across the country have allowed increasing numbers of single-parent, stepparent, and joint adoptions by homosexuals in recent years. This typically has occurred quietly, in the absence of any overall policy directives. Religious right activists have decried this trend. "It seems to have government saying that a gay environment is a good one to grow up in," a spokeswoman for the Family Research Council explains. The courts may see it differently. "Courts are more used to having to coerce people to take responsibility for and care for their children," a gay-rights activist notes, "and so when someone, anyone, comes in asking to be made responsible, they are very sympathetic."

In custody cases in states where sodomy has been illegal, homosexuals have in some cases been presumed to be criminals. As such, they have been considered unfit parents for their children. In 1994, for example, a Virginia court took custody of a toddler from his mother. The court awarded custody of the child to his grandmother. The decision was made only because the mother was a lesbian living with her same-sex partner. Courts have also cited homosexuality as reason for denying a biological parent custody in divorce cases. It has also been cited as reason for denying visitation rights to a nonbiological partner who'd raised a child from birth. Courts have also denied such a partner custody of the child when the biological parent has died.

In general, courts dealing with custody and visitation disputes have typically taken one of three approaches to a parent's homosexuality:

- The "per se" (meaning "in itself" or "intrinsic") approach presumes that all homosexuals are unfit parents.
- The "nexus" (meaning a "connection" or "link") approach considers a parent's homosexuality only if evidence shows that it is having an adverse effect on the child.
- The "presumption" approach doesn't find that homosexuality itself makes one an unfit parent but does presume that evidence of homosexuality in the child's home (such as the presence of a parent's same-sex partner) is not in the child's best interest.

In practice, even in states where the law requires the nexus approach, judges often decide against homosexual parents without any specific evidence of harm to the child. Many judges decide against homosexual parents on the grounds that living with an openly homosexual parent will harm the child by exposing the child to social disapproval of the parent's homosexuality.

FAMILY BENEFITS OF LEGAL MARRIAGE

Legal marriage comes with a host of benefits for spouses. In much the same ways, a child also benefits from having two legally married parents. Some benefits are the same as for married spouses. Those include inheritance rights, coverage from a parent's employer's health insurance plan, and so on. Other benefits are unique to children. Children benefit from having two parents with a legal right to take leave to care for a sick child, a legal obligation to support the child, and rights to custody and visitation. Schools, day-care centers, doctors' offices, and hospitals all typically require that only parents or legal guardians can make arrangements for children. This creates problems for a family with same-sex parents. For example, the legal parent must typically notify the school that it's OK for the other parent to pick up the child after class.

One of the strongest arguments for same-sex marriage is that it benefits the children. Regardless of whether one thinks homosexuality is sinful, extending the same benefits and protections enjoyed by the children of married, heterosexual couples to

IN SUPPORT OF SAME-SEX MARRIAGE

THE AMERICAN ACADEMY OF PEDIATRICS is an organization dedicated to the health and well-being of infants, children, adolescents, and young adults. It supports same-sex marriage:

"The American Academy of Pediatrics recognizes that a considerable body of professional literature provides evidence that children with parents who are homosexual can have the same advantages and the same expectations for health, adjustment, and development as can children whose parents are heterosexual. . . . Because these families and children need the permanence and security that are provided by having two fully sanctioned and legally defined parents, the Academy supports the legal adoption of children by co-parents or second parents. . . . In addition, legislative initiatives assuring legal status equivalent to marriage for gay and lesbian partners . . . can also attend to providing security and permanence for the children of those partnerships."

—STATEMENT BY THE AMERICAN ACADEMY OF PEDIATRICS, 2002

children of homosexuals helps them. For the hundreds of thousands of children living with homosexual parents, arguments about whether homosexual parents are "as good as" heterosexual parents are irrelevant. Like all children, they have the parents they have, not some theoretical ideal.

Same-sex marriage has potential benefits—and pitfalls—for families beyond those most directly involved. A same-sex weddings can bring family members together in celebration. Or it can drive them apart. Prospective brides or grooms sometimes ask family members to celebrate and call "marriage" a relationship they may not approve of or even recognize as a marriage. Same-sex marriage is also relevant to families with heterosexual parents and a homosexual child. The example of married same-sex couples

Mary Norton *(left)* and her partner, Wendy Baker *(right)*, share a glass of wine after exchanging vows during their wedding ceremony in Attleboro, Massachusetts. Their adopted children, Mickey Baker-Norton *(lower left)* and Hannah Baker-Norton *(lower right)*, Judge Donna Nesselbush *(second from left)*, and the Reverend Maryellen Butke *(second from right)* are looking on.

enables such families to envision a life for the child that includes marriage—a very important institution in the parents' lives.

BUT IS IT GOOD FOR THE CHILDREN?

Religious conservatives who oppose same-sex marriage often point to specific ill effects they believe same-sex parenting has on children. According to Focus on the Family's Glenn T. Stanton and Bill Maier, for example, "Much of the value mothers and fathers bring to their children is due to the fact that mothers and fathers are different. And by cooperating together and complementing each other in their differences, a mother and father team provided these good things that same-sex caregivers can't." The different parenting styles of men and women provide the benefit of difference—"diversity of experiences for children. . . . Fathers stimulate development of large motor skills, while mothers foster

FIRST-PERSON ACCOUNTS

FIRST-PERSON ACCOUNTS of growing up with homosexual parents vary:

"We constantly wonder if we will eventually become gay. There is humiliation when other kids see our parents kissing a same-sex lover in front of us. Trust me, it's hard on the children, no matter how much they love their gay parent."

—JAKII EDWARDS, ON GROWING UP IN A LESBIAN HOME, N.D.

"I was angry that I was not part of a 'normal' family and could not live with a 'normal' mother. I wondered what I did to deserve this."

—CAREY CONLEY, AGED TWENTY-ONE,
ADOPTED AND RAISED BY A LESBIAN, N.D.

"Nobody can say that their family is a real family and my family is just a bunch of people living in the same house."

—ELEVEN-YEAR-OLD ROBBIE BARNETT-KEMPER,
WHEN HIS MOTHERS MARRIED, IN CANADA, 2003

fine motor skills. Fathers push limits, mothers encourage security." Mothers and fathers "communicate differently" and manage discipline differently. "Fathers do 'man things' and women do 'lady things.'" Because they lack exposure to the full spectrum of male and female parenting, "children growing up in intentionally mother-only or father-only homes will suffer in terms of lack of confidence, independence and security. Boys and girls will be at greater risk for gender confusion, abuse and exploitation from other men. They will be less likely to have healthy respect for both women and men as they grow into adulthood."

Gay-family supporters counter that a lot more differences exist among men or women than between them. They also note that children are exposed to more adults than just their parents. And, they add, no scientific evidence proves any ill effects on children living with same-sex parents. Antihomosexual activists insist that ill effects are likely. They say that child welfare is too important to treat as a social experiment.

Many experts and studies do agree that children do better when they live in households with two parents. One-parent households generally have less money, and single parents have less time for supervision of their children. But there's little data comparing two-parent homosexual families with otherwise similar two-parent heterosexual families. None of that data indicates that a mom and dad are better for children than two moms or two dads.

The American Psychoanalytic Association, the National Association of Social Workers, the American Academy of Pediatrics, and the American Psychological Association have all affirmed that children raised by same-sex parents do as well as those raised by heterosexual parents. At Stanford University, Professor Michael Wald surveyed research studies of children with homosexual parents. He found no evidence of "emotional, intellectual, or social development problems because of their parents' sexual orientation." A review of studies by the American Psychological Association found that children raised by homosexual parents are not "disadvantaged in any significant respect relative to the children of heterosexual parents." In addition, there's ample evidence that children of homosexuals and children raised by homosexuals are no more likely to become homosexuals themselves than anyone else.

Some children living with same-sex parents do experience stigma—being teased or looked down upon—because of their parents' sexual orientation. However, almost all children experience stigma of one sort or another. No evidence shows any special ill effects from the stigma of having homosexual parents.

CHAPTER
SIX

Politics and Legal Developments in the 1990s

By 1990 couples in several states were talking with activist lawyers about same-sex marriage. They were looking for lawyers who would help them sue for the right to get married. Some lawyers who supported their cause turned them down. They believed the time was not yet right to push the issue. Three couples in Hawaii, though, found legal representation.

Ninia Baehr *(left)* and Genora Dancel *(right)* appear at a news conference on December 3, 1996, after a Hawaii state supreme court judge barred the state of Hawaii from denying marriage licenses to same-sex couples.

Together they pursued their case.

GOING TO COURT IN HAWAII

All three of those couples had applied for marriage licenses in 1990. All were refused. The couples were Ninia Baehr (whose name would identify the case) and Genora Dancel, Joe Mellilo and Pat Lagon, and Antoinette Pregil and Tammy Rodriguez.

A lower court ruled against the three couples in 1991. They then appealed to a higher court. On May 5, 1993, Hawaii's supreme court over-ruled the lower court's decision. The state supreme court noted that "marriage is a basic civil right." The court decided that it violated the state constitution to deny marriage licenses to same-sex couples unless the state could show a "compelling state interest" for doing so. The state supreme court sent the case back to a lower court for trial to determine whether the state had such a compelling reason.

The state supreme court's decision was primarily based on one clause in Hawaii's constitution. That clause prohibits discrimination because of "race, religion, sex, or ancestry." But the decision was also based on the U.S. Supreme Court's 1967 *Loving v. Virginia* decision. The *Loving* decision struck down state laws that banned interracial marriage. Legal arguments that bans on same-sex marriage are unconstitutional sex discrimination can only work in states that have such clauses in their constitutions. (There is no such clause in the U.S. Constitution.) Another legal precedent relevant to the *Baehr* case was a change in Hawaii's marriage laws, made by the state legislature in 1984. That change specified that the state could not deny marriage licenses because one or both of the persons was impotent (unable to have intercourse) or "physically incapable of entering into the marriage state."

Ironically, lawyers for the three couples in the *Baehr* case didn't even try to make a sex-discrimination argument at first. Lawyers for the state introduced the idea of sex discrimination. They argued that the state's refusal to allow same-sex marriage was not sex discrimination. The court rejected other arguments by the three couples' lawyers. They had argued that refusing to allow same-sex marriage violated the couples' rights to privacy and illegally discriminated against them on the basis of sexual orientation. The court decided that homosexuality wasn't legally relevant here. But the court said the issue of sex discrimination was.

The court held that Hawaii's state constitutional ban on sex discrimination required "strict scrutiny" of any discrimination against same-sex couples. The U.S. Supreme Court, and generally state courts as well, applies the "strict scrutiny" standard to laws that relate to "suspect classification." A "suspect" class or category is one against which discrimination is constitutionally forbidden (such as race or religion). Courts also generally give "strict scrutiny" to laws that infringe upon a "fundamental" right. (The *Loving* decision treated marriage as a fundamental right.) Laws given "strict scrutiny" by a court are struck down unless, as the Supreme Court put it in 1985, they are "narrowly tailored to further a compelling interest." (The U.S. Supreme Court does not consider sex or sexual orientation to be a "suspect classification," and the court hasn't designated any new "suspect classifications" since the mid-1970s.)

At the federal level and in many states, a law alleged to discriminate on the basis of sex is generally held to "intermediate scrutiny," less demanding than "strict scrutiny" but still requiring a good reason for the law to stand. The U.S. Supreme Court has found that for such a law to remain in force, it "must serve important governmental objectives and must be substantially related to the achievement of those objectives."

At the federal level, however, laws accused of discrimination on the basis of sexual orientation have generally been held only to "rational basis" scrutiny, which is even less demanding than "intermediate scrutiny." Under this standards, the law must be "rationally" related to a legitimate state interest, no matter how iffy that relationship is, and can be upheld even if the law itself does more harm than good. It's unlikely that any laws restricting same-sex marriage would be overturned by federal courts subjecting it only to "rational basis" scrutiny.

THE COURT'S DECISION ON THE *BAEHR* CASE

THE HAWAII SUPREME COURT did not find a violation of the right to privacy in the *Baehr* case. The court, instead, found a case of sexual discrimination:

"We conclude that the circuit court's order [against the three couples in the *Baehr* case] runs aground on the shoals of the Hawaii Constitution's equal protection clause and that, on the record before us, unresolved factual questions preclude entry of judgment. . . .

"We hold that the applicant couples do not have a fundamental constitutional right to same-sex marriage arising out of the right of privacy or otherwise.

"Our holding, however, does not leave the applicant couples without a potential remedy in this case. . . . The applicant couples are free to press their equal protection claim. If they are successful, the State of Hawaii will no longer be permitted to refuse marriage licenses to couples merely on the basis that they are of the same sex. . . .

"The applicant couples correctly contend that the [state's] refusal to allow them to marry on the basis that they are members of the same sex deprives them of access to a multiplicity of rights and benefits that are contingent upon that status. . . .

"We hold that sex is a 'suspect category' for purposes of equal protection analysis under . . . the Hawaii Constitution and that [the state's marriage statute] is subject to the 'strict scrutiny' test. It therefore follows, and we so hold, that (1) [the state's marriage statute] is presumed to be unconstitutional (2) unless . . . an agent of the State of Hawaii can show that (a) the statute's sex-based classification is justified by compelling state interests and (b) the statute is narrowly drawn to avoid unnecessary abridgements of the applicant couples' constitutional rights. . . .

"We vacate the circuit court's order and judgment and remand this matter for further proceedings consistent with this opinion."

—HAWAII SUPREME COURT DECISION IN *BAEHR V. LEWIN*, MAY 5, 1993

State courts following strict scrutiny, such as Hawaii's, are another matter. Hawaii's supreme court's decision in 1993 didn't actually legalize same-sex marriage in Hawaii. What it did was force the state and activists opposed to same-sex marriage to justify their position in court. The *Baehr* case continued its way through the state's courts. Eventually, on December 3, 1996, Judge Kevin Chang ruled that the state had failed to present "sufficient credible evidence that demonstrates that the public interest in the well-being of children and families, or the optimal development of children would be adversely affected by same-sex marriage. Nor has [the state] demonstrated how same-sex marriage would adversely affect the public fisc [the state treasury], the state interest in assuring recognition of Hawaii marriages in other states, the institution of marriage, or any other important public or governmental interest." Hawaii seemed poised to become the first U.S. state to legalize same-sex marriage.

BACKLASH

But as Judge Chang issued his ruling, a backlash against same-sex marriage was in full swing. Opponents of same-sex marriage from all over the United States poured millions of dollars into Hawaii. The money was to fund a campaign to change the state's constitution to outlaw same-sex marriage. The state appealed Judge Chang's decision. But before the state supreme court ruled on the matter, Hawaii's voters rendered the case moot (legally irrelevant). In November 1998, voters approved an amendment to Hawaii's state constitution. That amendment specified that the state's "legislature shall have the power to reserve marriage to opposite-sex couples."

A similar story played out in Alaska. There, the constitution not only forbids sex discrimination, as Hawaii's does. It also explicitly guarantees a right to privacy. Two gay men who were denied a marriage license in Alaska sued the state. In 1998 a state superior court judge, Peter Michalski, ruled that the "right to choose one's life partner" was constitutionally "fundamental" in

Alaska. "Government intrusion into the choice of a life partner encroaches on the intimate personal decisions of the individual," the judge continued. "The relevant question is not whether same-sex marriage is so rooted in our traditions that it is a fundamental right, but whether the freedom to choose one's own life partner is so rooted in our traditions." As in Hawaii, the judge sent the case back into the state court system for further hearings. Those hearings were to determine whether the state had a "compelling interest" in denying same-sex couples the right to marry. As in Hawaii, the Alaska court proceedings were rendered moot when Alaska's voters approved an amendment to the state's constitution in November 1998. That amendment banned same-sex marriage.

Much concern outside Hawaii about same-sex marriage following the *Baehr* decision focused on the "full faith and credit" clause of the U.S. Constitution: "Full faith and credit shall be given in each state to the public acts, records, and judicial proceedings of every state." In general, this clause compels states to recognize marriages licensed in other states. The clause is generally binding even if those marriages would not be permitted in the state granting such recognition. For example, only about half the states allow first cousins to marry. However, when cousins do marry in one of those states, all the other states recognize that marriage as valid. Likewise, states with different rules about how old you have to be to get married recognize one another's marriages. It was unclear whether the "full faith and credit" clause would compel other states to recognize same-sex marriages licensed in Hawaii. Might a same-sex couple living in Texas travel to Hawaii, get married, come home, and be legally married in Texas too?

The federal Defense of Marriage Act (DOMA) addressed such concerns. President Clinton, a Democrat, signed it into law in

THE DEFENSE OF MARRIAGE ACT

THE FEDERAL DEFENSE OF MARRIAGE ACT was signed into law by President Clinton in September 1996. It states:

"No State, territory, or possession of the United States, or Indian tribe, shall be required to give effect to any public act, record, or judicial proceeding of any other State, territory, possession, or tribe respecting a relationship between persons of the same sex that is treated as a marriage under the laws of such other State, territory, possession, or tribe, or a right or claim arising from such relationship. . . .

"In determining the meaning of any Act of Congress, or of any ruling, regulation, or interpretation of the various administrative bureaus and agencies of the United States, the word 'marriage' means only a legal union between one man and one woman as husband and wife, and the word 'spouse' refers only to a person of the opposite sex who is a husband or wife."

—THE DEFENSE OF MARRIAGE ACT, 1996

September 1996. This happened in the heat of his campaign for reelection. (His Republican opponent, Bob Dole, had signed a marriage protection pledge against same-sex marriage.) The Defense of Marriage Act forbids federal recognition and federal tax and pension benefits for same-sex marriage partners. It also gives states the right to refuse to recognize any same-sex marriages that might be performed in other states.

Good, commonsensical public-policy reasons exist for cooperating with other states' laws. (The legal term for this cooperation is comity.) Contracts with married people for insurance or mortgages, for example, need to remain in force wherever the couple happens to be. But states can make exceptions. The U.S. Supreme Court (in *Nevada v. Hall*, 1979) declared that the "full faith and credit clause does not require a state to apply another

Demonstrators in San Francisco, California, protest the proposed federal Defense of Marriage Act in June 1996.

state's law in violation of its own legitimate public policy." If state law or a state constitution makes it state policy to refuse to marry same-sex couples, then the state is on solid legal ground in refusing to recognize any such marriages licensed in other states.

While Congress was enacting DOMA, activists across the country were introducing bans on same-sex marriages in state legislatures and through voter referenda. Previously, no such explicit bans had existed. In February 1996, a coalition of groups opposed to same-sex marriage announced in Iowa, just before the state's nominating caucuses for presidential candidates, the Campaign to Protect Marriage. The coalition promised a "well-funded effort" to ban same-sex marriage at the state and federal levels. By the end of that year, fifteen state legislatures had enacted legislation against same-sex marriage.

THE DEBATE IN CONGRESS on the Defense of Marriage Act was extraordinarily passionate. Here's a sample:

"Dr. Martin Luther King, Jr., used to say when people talked about interracial marriage, and I quote, 'Races do not fall in love and get married. Individuals fall in love and get married.' I have known racism. I have known bigotry. This bill stinks of the same fear, hatred, and intolerance. It should not be called the Defense of Marriage Act. It should be called the defense of mean-spirited bigots act."

—REPRESENTATIVE JOHN LEWIS, DEMOCRAT FROM GEORGIA, A LONGTIME CIVIL RIGHTS ACTIVIST, 1996

This is not, as its critic have said, a "'hate-driven bill.' In fact, it is precisely the critics of [this bill], who are demanding that homosexuality be considered as just another lifestyle—these are the people who seek to force their agenda upon the vast majority of Americans who reject the homosexual lifestyle. [The Defense of Marriage Act] will safeguard the sacred institutions of marriage and the family from those who seek to destroy them and who are willing to tear apart America's moral fabric in the process. . . . It will establish a simple, clear federal definition of marriage as the legal union of one man and one woman, and it will exempt sovereign states from being compelled by a half-baked interpretation of the U.S. Constitution to recognize same-sex marriages wrongfully legalized in another state."

—SENATOR JESSE HELMS, REPUBLICAN OF NORTH CAROLINA, 1996

The following year, 1997, nine more states passed legislation against same-sex marriage. In 1998 six more did so (including Hawaii and Alaska), bringing the total to thirty.

At the same time, state and local gay-rights legislation, in general, came under fire across the nation following the *Baehr* decision. In 1994 Austin, Texas, became the first U.S. municipality to overturn an existing domestic-partnership law. Other local municipalities voted to undo previously enacted gay-rights laws.

VERMONT

In July 1997, three Vermont couples (a gay couple and two lesbian couples) who had been refused marriage licenses filed suit seeking the right to marry. Their case worked its way through state courts to the Vermont Supreme Court. On December 20, 1999, the court unanimously ruled that the state must grant gay and lesbian couples the same protections and benefits as heterosexual couples. The court said that the state must either allow same-sex marriage or create an equivalent domestic partnership option.

The court's decision, written by Chief Justice Jeffrey L. Amestoy, specified that "the issue before the Court . . . does not turn on the religious or moral debate over intimate same-sex relationships, but rather on the statutory exclusion of same-sex couples from the secular benefits and protections offered married couples." Judge Amestoy cited the "common benefits" clause of the Vermont state constitution as the basis for the court's decision. This clause states that the government is to serve the "common benefit" of all the state's citizens rather than the "particular . . . advantage" of just some of its citizens. The court found that "the extension of the Common Benefits Clause to acknowledge plaintiffs as Vermonters who seek nothing more, or less, than legal protection and security for their avowed commitment to an intimate and lasting human relationship is simply, when all is said and done, a recognition of our common humanity."

The court declared that the state of Vermont "is constitutionally required to extend to same-sex couples the common benefits and protections that flow from marriage under Vermont law. Whether this ultimately takes the form of inclusion within the marriage laws themselves or a parallel domestic partnership system or some equivalent statutory [legal] alternative, rests with the legislature."

Reaction to the court's decision was swift and, predictably, extreme. Gay-rights activists all over the United States hailed the decision as a milestone. Gary Bauer, a religious right conservative then running for U.S. president, said that the ruling was in some ways "worse than terrorism." The Family Research Council's Robert Knight said, "They [Vermont] did something very wrong, which was to impose marital-type benefits on non-marital relationships. That undermines the authority of marriage. It undermines its importance in society."

Debate on the issue—inside the Vermont State Legislature, throughout the state, and across the nation—was extensive and often heated. Ultimately, the legislature decided to meet the court's order by allowing same-sex couples to form "civil unions." A civil union would have a status exactly equivalent to

FINDINGS OF THE VERMONT LEGISLATURE

VERMONT'S CIVIL UNION LAW PROVIDES THE BENEFITS and protections of marriage but does not interfere with varying religious views of same-sex marriage:

"Extending the benefits and protections of marriage to same-sex couples through a system of civil unions preserves the fundamental constitutional right of each of the multitude of religious faiths in Vermont to choose freely and without state interference to whom to grant the religious status, sacrament, or blessing of marriage under the rules, practices, or traditions of such faith."

—FINDINGS OF THE VERMONT STATE LEGISLATIVE
COMMITTEE CONSIDERING SAME-SEX MARRIAGE, 2000

State Representative Bill Lippert *(right)* of Vermont congratulates Governor Howard Dean *(left)* after Dean signed the state's civil union bill into law in 2000. Lippert is a noted gay-rights activist in Vermont.

marriage as defined by Vermont's state law. But it would not be called a marriage. On April 26, 2000, Vermont's governor, Howard Dean, signed the civil union bill into law. The law took effect at midnight on July 1. Shortly after midnight, two women in Brattleboro became the first couple to be issued a license and joined in union under the law.

AFTERMATH

In the state of Vermont, 1,704 civil unions were performed between July 1 and December 31, 2000. By 2003 a total of 5,560 had been performed. Only 833 of these were Vermont couples. The others had come from all over the United States and Canada.

A few of these out-of-state couples later faced legal problems when their relationships failed and they decided to divorce. However, their home states didn't recognize their unions and therefore refused to dissolve them. A similar legal quandary greeted Vermont couples who moved to any of the states with laws against recognizing same-sex marriages. By the time Vermont began to allow civil unions for same-sex couples, thirty-five states had such laws. Also, none of the more than one thousand legal marital rights and benefits specified by the U.S. government applied to any of these couples, even if they remained in Vermont. The Defense of Marriage Act forbids it.

Carolyn Conrad *(right)* and Kathleen Peterson *(opposite Conrad)* exchange vows during their civil union ceremony in Brattleboro, Vermont. They were the first couple to enter a civil union in Vermont.

Couples joined in civil unions pose on the steps of the statehouse in Montpelier, Vermont, on April 25, 2001.

Same-sex marriage seemed to be moving in two directions at once in the aftermath of Vermont's civil union law. The Vermont law was a big step forward for same-sex marriage. But laws were still being enacted in other states forbidding it. Meanwhile, public acceptance of same-sex marriage seemed to be increasing. The *New York Times* began printing announcements of same-sex civil unions in August 2002. By then, more than 70 other U.S. newspapers were already doing so for same-sex civil unions, partnership registrations, or commitment ceremonies. By the end of that year, 180 papers were printing such announcements.

Changing attitudes toward same-sex marriage showed a sharp generational tilt. In 2000 only 25 percent of people older than sixty-five supported same-sex marriage. At the same time, 60 percent of those between eighteen and twenty-nine supported it. Was same-sex marriage a wave of the future?

CHAPTER
SEVEN

Massachusetts and Beyond

Same-sex marriage is well established in many other countries. In Canada, most of northern Europe, and a scattered assortment of other countries either legal marriage or equivalent domestic partnership arrangements are available to same-sex couples. In these places, homosexual sex between consenting adults is legal. In much of the United States, until quite recently, it hasn't been.

British couple Celia Kitzinger *(left)* and Sue Wilkinson *(right)* were legally married in British Columbia, Canada, in 2003. In the United Kingdom, where the couple lives, they only qualify for civil partnership. In 2006 Kitzinger and Wilkinson took their case to court to challenge British law on same-sex marriage.

LAWRENCE V. TEXAS

As recently as 1986, the U.S. Supreme Court had upheld a Georgia law against sodomy in *Bowers v. Hardwick*. Police had arrested a man for having sex with another man in his own bedroom. The Court asserted that homosexual sex between consenting adults in their own home was not protected by a constitutional right to privacy, although marital sex was.

But on June 26, 2003, the Court reversed its decision.

A DIVIDED SUPREME COURT

"What are you doing in my bedroom?"

—MICHAEL HARDWICK, SPEAKING TO A POLICE OFFICER ABOUT TO ARREST HIM FOR HAVING SEX WITH ANOTHER MAN IN HIS OWN HOME, 1982

AFTER BEING CHARGED WITH VIOLATING the Georgia statute criminalizing sodomy by having sex with another adult male in the bedroom of his home, Michael Hardwick challenged the constitutionality of the statute. The U.S. Supreme Court ruled that:

"The Constitution does not confer a fundamental right upon homosexuals to engage in sodomy. None of the fundamental rights announced in this Court's prior cases involving family relationships, marriage, or procreation bear any resemblance to the right asserted in this case. . . .

"The fact that homosexual conduct occurs in the privacy of the home does not affect the result."

—U.S. SUPREME COURT, *BOWERS V. HARDWICK*, 1986

A Dissenting Opinion

However, four of the Supreme Court's nine justices sharply disagreed with the majority opinion in *Bowers*. They thought the case was about the constitutional right to privacy. "This case is about 'the most comprehensive of rights and the right most valued by civilized men,' namely, 'the right to be let alone. . . .' The Court claims that its decision today merely refuses to recognize a fundamental right to engage in homosexual sodomy; what the Court really has refused to recognize is the fundamental interest all individuals have in controlling the nature of their intimate associations with others. . . . Indeed, the right of an individual to conduct intimate relationships in the intimacy of his or her home seems to me to be the heart of the Constitution's protection of privacy."

—JUSTICE HARRY BLACKMUN, WRITING FOR THE FOUR DISSENTING JUSTICES, 1986

Lawrence v. Texas struck down all the sodomy laws remaining on the books in the states that still had them, about one-third of the states. Writing for the Court, Justice Anthony Kennedy asserted that "the petitioners," who had challenged the state of Texas's sodomy law, "are entitled to respect for their private lives. The state cannot demean their existence to control their destiny by making their private sexual conduct a crime."

In the context of the ongoing debate about same-sex marriage, the *Lawrence* decision was a bombshell. It completely eliminated any argument against same-sex marriage based on the fact that, in some states, the sex that those partners would presumably engage in was illegal.

MASSACHUSETTS

In April 2001, lawyers filed suit in Boston on behalf of seven same-sex couples seeking the right to marry in Massachusetts. (Included in the group were Hillary and Julie Goodridge. Their jointly adopted name would identify the case.) The trial court, as expected, ruled against them. The couples appealed. The case made its way to the Massachusetts Supreme Judicial Court. On November 18, 2003, the court ruled that the state had "failed to identify any constitutionally adequate reason for denying civil marriage to same-sex couples." It asserted that "the right to marry means little if it does not include the right to marry the person of one's choice." The court specifically cited the U.S. Supreme Court's 1967 decision in *Loving v. Virginia*: "In this case, as in . . . *Loving*, a statute deprives individuals of access to an institution of fundamental legal, personal, and social significance—the institution of marriage—because of a single trait: skin color in . . . *Loving*, sexual orientation here. As it did in . . . *Loving*, history must yield to a more fully developed understanding of the invidious quality of the discrimination." The court required the state to start issuing marriage licenses to same-sex couples within 180 days. The deadline was May 17, 2004.

Following the court's decision, the governor of Massachusetts, Mitt Romney, said he'd lead efforts to amend the state constitution to block same-sex marriage. But unlike Hawaii, where the constitutional amendment procedure moves quickly, it takes two years in Massachusetts to get a constitutional amendment on the ballot for voters to approve or disapprove. Same-sex-marriage advocates would have time to counter the backlash against the *Goodridge* decision. It would help these advocates greatly that homosexuals were well enough tolerated in communities throughout Massachusetts to be open with their neighbors about their sexual orientation. Homosexuals and therefore gay marriage were not viewed as so alien in Massachusetts as they might be in places where people had less direct experience with openly homosexual neighbors.

Opponents of same-sex marriage did propose amending the state's constitution to ban it. And in February 2004, the state legislature passed an amendment declaring marriage in Massachusetts to be between one man and one woman only. The

EQUALITY UNDER LAW

THE MASSACHUSETTS STATE CONSTITUTION specifically forbids discrimination based on sex, race, color, or national origin. It states:

"All people are born free and equal and have certain natural, essential and unalienable rights; among which may be reckoned the right of enjoying and defending their lives and liberties. . . . Equality under law shall not be denied or abridged because of sex, race, color, creed or national origin."

—MASSACHUSETTS STATE CONSTITUTION

SEPARATE IS NOT EQUAL

THE SUPREME JUDICIAL COURT OF MASSACHUSETTS advised the state legislature that limiting same-sex couples to civil unions—rather than marriage—would violate the state's constitution:

"Because the proposed [civil union] law by its express terms forbids same-sex couples entry into civil marriage, it continues to relegate same-sex couples to a different status. . . . For no rational reason the marriage laws of the Commonwealth [of Massachusetts] discriminated against a defined class; no amount of tinkering with language will eradicate that stain. The [proposed civil union] bill would have the effect of maintaining and fostering a stigma of exclusion that the Constitution prohibits. . . . The history of our nation has demonstrated that separate is seldom, if ever, equal."

—CLARIFICATION TO *GOODRIDGE V. DEPARTMENT OF PUBLIC HEALTH*, ISSUED BY THE SUPREME JUDICIAL COURT OF MASSACHUSETTS, FEBRUARY 2004

amendment would have to be reapproved by the legislature in 2005 before being put on the ballot in 2006, at the earliest. But ultimately, unlike in Hawaii, this amendment went nowhere.

The legislature also discussed creating a civil union option for same-sex partners. The state senate asked the Massachusetts Supreme Judicial Court whether such a measure would meet the requirements of the *Goodridge* decision. The court said nothing short of marriage would do. Massachusetts prepared to become the first U.S. state to grant marriage licenses to same-sex couples in exactly the same way it does to heterosexual couples.

REACTION TO MASSACHUSETTS

Reaction to the *Goodridge* decision was strong—and loud—nationally. In late 2003 and 2004, President George W. Bush was seeking reelection. He and other Republicans were also hoping to

Demonstrators both for and against same-sex marriage held signs on the steps in front of the statehouse in Boston, Massachusetts, on March 11, 2004, while legislators debated the issue.

retain control of Congress in the November 2004 elections. Keeping the issue of same-sex marriage in the forefront of national politics was useful to Republican politicians. Their opposition to same-sex marriage shored up Republican support among conservative Christian voters. It also distracted attention from the increasingly unpopular war in Iraq.

In early 2004, President Bush and a host of other Republican politicians announced their support for a Federal Marriage Amendment to the U.S. Constitution. It was to read: "Marriage in the United States shall consist only of the union of a man and a woman. Neither this Constitution, nor the constitution of any State, shall be construed to require that marriage or the legal incidents thereof be conferred upon any union other than the union of a man and a woman." The intention of this amendment was to override both the Vermont and Massachusetts court decisions. The amendment would also forestall similar decisions in other states. State legislatures would still be free to enact laws defining same-sex civil unions or domestic partnerships. But they would not be able to legalize same-sex marriage.

At the same time, cases similar to *Goodridge* were working their way through courts in several other states. But at the local level, a handful of public offi-

In February 2004, during the year he was running for reelection, President George W. Bush announced that he would back the Federal Marriage Amendment, a constitutional amendment banning gay marriage.

cials decided not to wait. In San Francisco, Mayor Gavin Newsom announced on February 12, 2004, that he would issue marriage licenses to same-sex couples. More than four thousand such couples took out licenses there in the next four weeks. The first to be married were Del Martin, aged eighty-three, and Phyllis Lyon, aged seventy-nine, longtime lesbian-rights activists. They had been partners for more than fifty years. On March 11, the California Supreme Court suspended the issuing of any more

On August 12, 2004, Stuart Gaffney *(left)* and John Lewis *(right)* protested the California Supreme Court ruling that voided same-sex marriage licenses signed by San Francisco mayor Gavin Newsom.

marriage licenses to same-sex couples On August 12, the court annulled all the same-sex marriages that had been performed.

Meanwhile, other local officials across the country were taking similar action:

• A clerk in San-doval County, New Mexico, gave out marriage licenses to sixty-two same-sex couples on February 20. The state's attorney general ordered a stop to it later that day.

• On February 24, Mayor Jason West of New Paltz, New York, began marrying same-sex couples until, ordered by a court, he stopped doing so in March.

• On March 3, Multnomah County, Oregon, began to issue marriage licenses to same-sex couples. More than three thousand such couples received licenses before a county circuit judge ordered the county to stop issuing them seven weeks later.

On May 17, 2004, seventeen hundred marriage licenses were issued to same-sex couples in the state of Massachusetts. More than 250 same-sex couples had lined up at midnight to be the first in line for marriage licenses at city hall in Cambridge, Massachusetts. The phenomenon merited news coverage for a day or so, and then it faded. Same-sex marriage rapidly came to seem normal enough not to be newsworthy.

In July 2004, the Federal Marriage Amendment was voted down in the U.S. Senate. But overall, different factions in the United States still seemed to be pulling in opposite directions on same-sex marriage. Election Day in November 2004 was a bitter

Hillary *(left)* and Julie Goodridge *(right)* are pronounced "married" by the Reverend William Sinkford during their ceremony in Boston, Massachusetts, on May 17, 2004. (Their last name identified the landmark 2003 Massachusetts court decision.)

DISMANTLING THE BERLIN WALL

EVELYNN HAMMOND DESCRIBES HOW SHE FELT after receiving a license to marry her partner, Alexandra:

"As I walked to my office, I thought nothing will ever be the same, and yet picking up the [marriage] license was the same experience anyone straight would have had. I wish I had adequate words to describe all the events of last week, but I don't yet. My feelings aren't really about the personal aspects of same-sex marriage. I don't feel any different about Alexandra or my commitment to her than I did before last week. It is the historic aspect of this that feels strange, pleasant, and disquieting. I keep ruminating on what it means to be 'normal' versus 'not normal'; 'different' and 'not-different.' I feel like I was a part of the dismantling of the Berlin Wall—the dismantling of something that was literally both concrete and ideological."

—EVELYNN HAMMOND, MARRIED IN MASSACHUSETTS IN 2004

time for same-sex marriage advocates. The Republican Party, which had made opposition to same-sex marriage a central part of its agenda, made gains at the local, state, and national levels. Republicans won reelection to the White House and control of both the U.S. Senate and the House of Representatives. Voters in eleven states approved state constitutional amendments against same-sex marriage. Some of these amendments were so broadly worded as to threaten existing government-sponsored domestic partnership arrangements or forestall future ones.

At the same time, though, polls showed that growing numbers of people across the United States supported civil unions or same-sex marriage. National polls of voters in the November 2004 election showed that 37 percent said "there should be no legal recognition" of same-sex couples. But 35 percent favored same-sex civil unions. And 25 percent favored same-sex marriage. Taken together, well over half of those polled supported some form of legal recognition (civil union or marriage) for same-sex relationships. That indicated a 50 percent increase since the 2000 election. If civil unions weren't given as an option, 42 percent of those polled said that same-sex marriage should be legally recognized. That figure was up from 34 percent in 2000 and 27 percent in 1996.

During the next two years, several more states passed laws or constitutional amendments against same-sex marriage. But in 2006, renewed efforts in Congress to pass an amendment to the U.S. Constitution against same-sex marriage once again failed. And two states, Connecticut and New Jersey, created civil union options for same-sex couples similar to Vermont's. In early 2007, New Hampshire created a similar civil-union option for its

Demonstrators at a rally in San Francisco in October 2006. Homosexuals and supporters of same-sex marriage continue the fight for equality under the law.

OPINIONS—PRO AND CON

"I BELIEVE MARRIAGE IS BETWEEN A MAN AND A WOMAN, and I believe we ought to codify that one way or the other, and we have lawyers looking at the best way to do that."

—PRESIDENT GEORGE W. BUSH, JULY 2003

"How does the fact that two men live together in a loving relationship and commit themselves in Hawaii threaten your marriage in Florida or wherever? And the answer is always, well, it does not threaten my marriage, it threatens the institution of marriage. That . . . baffles me some. Institutions do not marry. . . . People marry."

—OPENLY GAY REPRESENTATIVE BARNEY FRANK
(DEMOCRAT–MASSACHUSETTS), 1996

"Legalization of same-sex marriage in Massachusetts "was also an outrage to the Massachusetts Constitution and to government of the people, by the people, and for the people. It was an act of judicial tyranny at the behest of an activist minority group."

—PETER SPRIGG OF THE FAMILY RESEARCH COUNCIL, 2004

"It was so cool. . . . I always accepted that 'Yeah, they're my moms,' but they were actually getting married. I felt thick inside with happiness. Just thick."

—GABRIEL, THIRTEEN, WHOSE PARENTS MARRIED
AT SAN FRANCISCO'S CITY HALL, MARCH 2004

residents. Rhode Island declared it would recognize any marriage legally made in any other state, including same-sex marriages made in neighboring Massachusetts.

As of the end of 2007, the state of legal recognition of same-sex marriage in the United States was mixed. Massachusetts remained the only state where marriage of same-sex couples was legally recognized. Out-of-state same-sex couples were not being issued marriage licenses there. Civil unions legally equivalent to marriage according to state law were available to same-sex couples in Vermont, Connecticut, New Jersey, and New Hampshire.

Twenty-seven states had constitutions with language defining marriage as a union between one man and one woman. Forty-one states had laws (rather than or in addition to constitutional amendments) against recognition of same-sex marriage. Same-sex marriages and civil unions enacted in other states are not legally recognized in any of these states. Only New Mexico, New York, New Jersey, Vermont, Massachusetts, Connecticut, and Rhode Island had neither a constitutional amendment nor state legislation against same-sex marriage. Legal recognition of other states' same-sex marriages and unions varied in those states and among localities within those states.

Also by the end of 2007, efforts had been mounted in several states to repeal previously passed constitutional amendments or legislation against recognition of same-sex marriage. But the U.S. Defense of Marriage Act remained in force. The U.S. government did not recognize any of the state-ordained same-sex legal arrangements. None of those arrangements entitled the couples involved to any of the federally defined benefits or privileges of marriage.

Same-sex marriage remains a hot issue—and a legal muddle for same-sex couples. The only clear trend is in public opinion. The U.S. public has, since the 1970s, consistently become increasingly tolerant of homosexuality. Will this tolerance ultimately lead to equal marriage rights for same-sex couples everywhere?

WHAT'S YOUR OPINION?

"Does prohibiting homosexual marriage violate some principle of 'equality' or 'justice'? Or does allowing it violate the very order of nature?"

—PETER SPRIGG OF THE FAMILY RESEARCH COUNCIL, 2004

"One of the main protections that come with marriage is the word marriage, which brings clarity and security that is simply not replaceable by any other word or by a sheaf of documents."

—SAME-SEX MARRIAGE ACTIVIST EVAN WOLFSON, 2004

"The conservative course is not to banish gay people from making such commitments. It is to expect that they make such commitments. We shouldn't just allow gay marriage. We should insist on gay marriage."

—CONSERVATIVE *NEW YORK TIMES* COLUMNIST DAVID BROOKS, 2003

Thomas Macaulay, an English historian and author, wrote, "[People] are never so likely to settle a question rightly as when they discuss it freely." In a democracy, the free exchange of ideas is not only encouraged, it's vital. Examining and discussing public issues and understanding opposing ideas are desirable and necessary elements of a free nation's ability to govern itself. Critical thinking is a valuable tool to use throughout life.

This book has helped you develop an understanding and appreciation of the complexity of the issue of same-sex marriage. You've read the opinions of many people who are either for or against same-sex marriage. The quotations on the previous page reflect three differing viewpoints about the same-sex marriage issue. Even the two quotes from conservative writers Peter Sprigg and David Brooks express opposing points of view.

Now it's time to do your own critical thinking and to begin forming your own opinion. Is the institution of marriage limited to a union between a man and a woman? Or should marriage be extended to any two people who love each other and are committed to spending the rest of their lives together? Is marriage an institution derived from God, from the state, or from both? Is childbearing and raising a family one of the purposes of marriage? What's your opinion—and why?

WHO'S WHO?

GEORGE W. BUSH was born in 1946 and served as governor of Texas from 1995 to 2000. He was elected president of the United States in 2000 and again in 2004. He is the son of former president George H. W. Bush, who served as U.S. president from 1989 to 1993. George W. Bush has gone on record as opposing the legal recognition of same-sex marriages, but he has done little to change policies related to homosexuality during his terms in office. He did, however, support the proposed Federal Marriage Amendment in 2004–2006, which would have prevented any state from allowing same-sex marriage and possibly civil unions as well. The amendment was defeated in the U.S. Senate.

BILL CLINTON was born in 1946 and became the forty-second president of the United States in 1993. He was reelected in 1996. During his presidential campaign, he promised to allow openly homosexual men and women to serve in the armed forces. However, this met with opposition and, ultimately, a compromise was agreed upon: the controversial "Don't Ask, Don't Tell" policy. This policy allows homosexuals to serve in the armed forces as long as they do not reveal their orientation to anyone. Clinton also signed the Defense of Marriage Act in 1996, which stated that individual states do not have to recognize same-sex marriages performed in other states.

HOWARD DEAN was born in 1948. He is a medical doctor who became active in Vermont politics. He was elected to the Vermont House of Representatives in 1982 and was elected lieutenant governor in 1986. He became governor when Richard Snelling, the former governor, died in office in 1991. Dean was elected to five two-year terms, serving as governor from 1991 to 2003. He was a contender for the Democratic presidential nomination in 2004 but ultimately lost the nomination to John Kerry. He was elected chairman of the Democratic National Committee in February 2005.

In 2000 the Vermont Supreme Court decided that excluding same-sex marriages was unconstitutional and ordered the state legislature to either allow such marriages or to create a similar status. Dean then faced calls to amend the state constitution to prohibit either option. He chose to support the second option. Howard Dean signed the nation's first civil union legislation into law in 2000, making Vermont the first state in the nation to allow civil unions.

JAMES DOBSON was born in 1936. Dobson is the founder and chairperson of the organization Focus on the Family, an evangelical organization that works with Christian churches to promote socially conservative laws and policies, including strong opposition to same-sex marriage. Dobson is an influential member of the modern American evangelical movement. He produces a conservative, daily radio program through Focus and has authored numerous books.

JERRY FALWELL was born in 1933 and was an influential spiritual leader and one of the leaders of the modern American evangelical Christian movement. After graduating in 1956 from Baptist Bible College in Springfield, Missouri, Falwell went on to found the Thomas Road Baptist Church that same year at the age of twenty-two. Falwell served as senior pastor at Thomas Road until his death in 2007.

In 1971 Falwell founded Liberty University, a Christian liberal arts university in Lynchburg, Virginia, and in 1979, he helped found the Moral Majority, a political organization for evangelical Christians. The Moral Majority campaigned on a number of issues central to the modern evangelical movement, including opposition to state recognition of same-sex marriage. The organization, which was officially dissolved in 1989, inspired the creation of similar groups. Falwell had strong ties to the Republican Party, and he is credited with helping Ronald Reagan win the presidency in the 1980 election.

BARNEY FRANK was born in 1940. Frank is a member of the U.S. House of Representatives. He is a Democrat representing Massachusetts's 4th Congressional District. Frank attended Harvard University as an undergraduate and as a law student. In 1980 he was elected to the U.S. Congress to fill the seat of a retiring member, and in 1982, he won his first full term. Since then he has been reelected in every election by a wide margin.

Frank first spoke openly about his own homosexuality in 1987. Since then he has been a prominent and vocal supporter of the gay-rights movement. In 1998 he founded the National Stonewall Democrats, the main national gay, lesbian, and bisexual Democratic organization. As of 2007, he was one of only two openly gay members in Congress.

ROCK HUDSON, born in 1925, was a popular American film actor for much of the 1950s and 1960s. He came to prominence playing romantic lead roles in both comedies and dramas. In his off-screen life, he was a closeted homosexual. He wed his agent's daughter in 1955, but the two divorced after only three years. After years of heavy smoking and drinking, Hudson's health deteriorated throughout the late 1970s and into the 1980s. In 1985 he revealed that he had contracted AIDS and was already in the late stages of the disease. He died shortly thereafter, but his public admission helped bring national attention and public sympathy to what was then a poorly understood disease.

GAVIN NEWSOM was born in 1967. He was elected mayor of San Francisco, California, in 2004. Little more than a month after he took office, Newsom issued a directive to the city–county clerk to allow marriage licenses for same-sex couples. Newsom stated that his decision was a reaction to hearing President George W. Bush's inaugural address in 2004, in which Bush reiterated his opposition to same-sex marriages. The weddings were halted by the California Supreme Court one month later, and all four thousand licenses granted to same-sex couples during this period were later voided.

TONY PERKINS, born in 1963, is a graduate of Jerry Falwell's Liberty University and became the president of the Family Research Council (FRC) in 2003. The FRC is a prominent conservative Christian lobbying organization closely connected to

James Dobson's group, Focus on the Family. As the head of the FRC, Perkins has supported numerous issues central to the modern evangelical movement, including opposition to same-sex marriage.

TROY PERRY was born in 1940 and became a Baptist minister at the age of fifteen. In 1959 he married his pastor's daughter and together they had two sons before Perry came out as a gay man in 1964. Perry and his wive divorced, and he left the ministry. In 1968, prompted by witnessing a friend's arrest during a police raid at a gay bar, Perry formed a congregation that would become the Metropolitan Community Church (MCC). The church has been a pioneer among Christian denominations in its openness to the gay community. Perry retired from the MCC in 2005 but remains active in gay-rights efforts. A film about his life, *Call Me Troy*, was released in 2007.

RONALD REAGAN, born in 1911, became a popular Hollywood movie actor. He served as governor of California from 1966 until 1974 and was elected president of the United States in 1980 and again in 1984. Among the many major issues that arose during his presidency was the beginning of the AIDS/HIV crisis. Reagan and his administration have been criticized for their slow response to the AIDS crisis. Although scientists first identified the disease in 1981, Reagan did not mention it publicly until 1985.

Reagan's stance on gayrights remains controversial. He and his administration opposed most gay-rights legislation and supported the existing criminal bans on homosexual acts. Yet Reagan was a close friend of Rock Hudson through his work in film and television. While governor of California, Reagan publicly opposed an initiative that would have forbidden homosexuals from working in public schools. Reagan died in 2004 of Alzheimer's disease.

ANDREW SULLIVAN is a prominent conservative political author and commentator who was born in 1963. He has worked at the *New Republic, Time*, and *Atlantic Monthly* magazines and is currently writing a regular weblog and a column for the Sunday *Times* (London). Sullivan is gay and, although he generally supports conservative points of view, he also strongly supports the legalization of same-sex marriage. He has argued that the Republican Party in the United States has abandoned true conservative political positions in favor of hot-button issues, such as same-sex marriage and the War on Terrorism (a war initiated by U.S. president George W. Bush in response to the September 11, 2001, terrorist attacks on the United States. The U.S. Congress authorized the war, which aims to curb the spread of terrorism.). This stand has brought Sullivan into conflict with other major conservative commentators.

1969 On June 28, New York City police raid the Stonewall Inn, a bar catering to homosexuals, in New York City. The riots and demonstrations that follow mark the beginning of the modern gay-rights movement.

1970 Two men, with their minister's blessing, apply for and are refused a marriage license in Minnesota.

1974 The American Psychiatric Association removes homosexuality from its list of medical diseases and disorders.

1981 First reports of a mysterious, deadly sickness afflicting gay men in the United States surfaced—the beginning of the AIDS epidemic.

1984 Berkeley, California, grants same-sex partners of local government employees the same benefits granted to their employees' legal spouses.

1986 The U.S. Supreme Court, in *Bowers v. Hardwick*, upholds state laws against homosexual sex.

1992 The software company Lotus becomes the first company with publicly traded stock to offer family benefits to same-sex partners of employees.

1993 On May 5, Hawaii's state supreme court, in *Baehr v. Lewin*, decides that it is a violation of the state constitution to deny marriage licenses to same-sex couples unless the state can show a "compelling state interest" for doing so.

Vermont becomes the first state to grant health insurance benefits to same-sex partners of state employees.

Austin, Texas, becomes the first U.S. municipality to overturn an existing domestic partnership law.

A Virginia court takes custody of a toddler, Tyler Bottoms, away from his mother and awards him to his grandmother solely because the mother is a lesbian living with her same-sex partner.

1996 In February a coalition of groups opposed to same-sex marriage announce a "well-funded effort" to ban gay marriage at the state and federal levels.

In September President Bill Clinton signs the Defense of Marriage Act, which forbids federal recognition and federal tax and pension benefits for same-sex marriage partners and gives states the right to refuse to recognize any same-sex marriages that might be performed in other states.

Fifteen states enact legislation against same-sex marriage.

1997 In July three Vermont couples (a gay couple and two lesbian couples) who had been refused marriage licenses file suit seeking the right to marry.

Nine more states pass legislation against same-sex marriage.

1998 An Alaska court renders a decision similar to Hawaii's 1993 *Baehr* decision, ruling that denying same-sex couples marriage licenses violates the state constitution.

In November voters in Hawaii and Alaska approve amendments to their state's constitution against same-sex marriage, effectively overruling the previous state court decisions favoring it. Six states pass antigay marriage legislation, bringing the total number of states that have done so to thirty.

1999   California sets up a domestic partnership registry, specifying only a few benefits associated with it, such as the right to visit a partner in the hospital as next of kin.

On December 20, Vermont's state supreme court rules that the state must grant same-sex couples the same protections and benefits as heterosexual couples, either by allowing same-sex marriage or by creating an equivalent domestic partnership option.

2000   Almost 600,000 same-sex couples are counted by the U.S. Census Bureau. Children are living in 28 percent of these households.

On April 26, Vermont's governor, Howard Dean, signs the state's civil union bill into law.

On July 1, shortly after midnight, two women in Brattleboro, Vermont, become the first couple to be issued a license and joined in union under the state's civil union law. By the end of the year, 1,704 such unions will be performed.

2001   In April lawyers file suit in Boston on behalf of seven same-sex couples seeking the right to marry in Massachusetts.

2003   On June 26, the U.S. Supreme Court, in *Lawrence v. Texas*, effectively strikes down all the remaining sodomy laws.

In September California's governor, Gray Davis, signs a bill assigning a long list of benefits and responsibilities to domestic partners, making registering for domestic partnership in the state similar to getting married in its statewide legal effects.

On November 18, the Massachusetts State Supreme Judicial Court rules, in *Goodridge v. Department of Public Health*, that denying marriage to same-sex couples violates the state constitution.

2004

On February 4, the Massachusetts State Supreme Judicial Court informs the state's legislature that a same-sex civil union law won't meet the court's mandate in the *Goodridge* decision and that nothing short of marriage will do.

On February 12, San Francisco mayor Gavin Newsom announces that he will start issuing marriage licenses to same-sex couples.

On February 20, a clerk in Sandoval County, New Mexico, gives out marriage licenses to same-sex couples. The state's attorney general orders a stop to it later that day.

On February 24, President George W. Bush announces his support for a federal amendment to the U.S. Constitution against same-sex marriage .

On February 24, Mayor Jason West of New Paltz, New York, begins marrying same-sex couples. Eventually, ordered by a court, he stops doing so.

On March 3, Multnomah County, Oregon, issues marriage licenses to same-sex couples. A county circuit judge orders the county to stop seven weeks later.

On March 11, the California State Supreme Court suspends the issuing of marriage licenses to same-sex couples.

On May 17, the first marriage licenses are issued to same-sex couples in Massachusetts.

In July the Family Marriage Amendment is voted down in the U.S. Senate.

On August 12, the California State Supreme Court annuls all the same-sex marriages that had been performed in San Francisco.

2005 On October 1, Connecticut legalizes same-sex civil unions, the same benefits and privileges the state grants to married couples. The legislature acted without being compelled to do so by any court.

2006 On June 7, the U.S. Senate once again votes against an amendment to the U.S. Constitution against same-sex marriage.

On October 25, the New Jersey Supreme Court rules that within six months the state must make available to same-sex couples legal recognition equivalent to marriage.

In December New Jersey's state legislature legalizes same-sex civil unions, making them equivalent to marriage under state law.

2007

In February Rhode Island declares that it will recognize any marriage legally made in another state, including same-sex marriages made in neighboring Massachusetts.

On April 26, New Hampshire's state legislature authorizes same-sex civil unions equivalent to marriage.

GLOSSARY

AIDS (acquired immunodeficiency syndrome): the disease caused by the human immunodeficiency virus (HIV), which attacks and destroys the kinds of white blood cells that are responsible for fighting off the body's exposure to infection. The weakened immune system leads to potentially life-threatening infections, including pneumonia and tuberculosis.

celibacy: abstinence from sexual intercourse

civil rights: the rights guaranteed to all citizens, established by the Constitution, the 13th and 14th amendments in particular, especially as applied to individuals

civil union: union between two people that confers the same legal rights as married couples; an alternative to same-sex marriage

commitment ceremony: a method for a same-sex couple to declare their intentions to love, honor, and care for each other when they are not able to marry; not legally binding and oftentimes a nonreligious ceremony

discrimination: treating a person differently based on a specified trait (such as race or sexual orientation) rather than individual merit

domestic partnership: a committed couple living together without being married

domestic partnership arrangements: benefits granted to a couple in a domestic partnership

fundamentalist Christians: those who believe that the Bible is literally true. Politically, they support the Defense of Marriage Act, antiabortion laws, prayer in schools, and traditional family values.

heterosexual: a person who has sexual attraction to members of the opposite sex

HIV (human immunodeficiency virus): a virus that attacks and disables the body's immune system causing AIDS

homophobia: fear and dislike of homosexuals

homosexual: sexual attraction to members of the same sex

monogamy: being married to one person at a time

"natural" marriage: the idea that marriage is an institution created by God and is defined as a union between a man and a woman

next of kin: person who is most closely related to an individual, either by blood or through legal recognition

polygamy: a marriage in which one spouse of either sex may have more than one mate

promiscuity: casual sex with more than one partner

revisionist scholars: those who put forth new interpretations of history or religious scripture

same-sex marriage: a legal and sometimes religious union between two people of the same sex with all the same legal benefits and privileges granted to a heterosexual union

sexual orientation: the direction of an individual's sexuality; the gender to which a person is sexually attracted

sodomy: anal or oral sex

traditional marriage: the union between one man and one woman

SOURCE NOTES

7 Ray Boylan, correspon-
dence with author, 1998.

8 Davina Kotulski, *Why You
Should Give a Damn about
Gay Marriage* (Los Angeles:
Advocate Books, 2004), 30.

10 Glenn T. Stanton and Bill
Maier, *Marriage on Trial: The
Case against Same-Sex
Marriage and Parenting*
(Downers Grove, IL:
Intervarsity Press, 2004), 21.

11 William N. Eskridge Jr. *The
Case for Same Sex Marriage:
From Sexuality to Liberty to
Civilized Commitment* (New
York: Free Press, 1996), 115.

20 David E. Newton, *Gay and
Lesbian Rights: A Reference
Handbook* (Santa Barbara,
CA: ABC-CLIO, 1994), 44.

20 George Chauncey, *Why
Marriage? The History Shaping
Today's Debate over Gay
Equality* (New York: Basic
Books, 2004), 147–148.

35 *New York Times*, November
17, 1998.

35 Macky Alston, "My
Blessed Gay Marriage,"
Beliefnet, 2007, http://www
.beliefnet.com, quoted in
David G. Myers and Letha

Dawson Scanzoni, *What
God Has Joined Together? A
Christian Case for Gay
Marriage* (New York:
HarperCollins, 2005), 132.

37 Kotulski, 108–109.

32 Stanton and Maier, 23.

42 Peter Sprigg, *Outrage: How
Gay Activists and Liberal
Judges Are Trashing
Democracy to Redefine
Marriage* (Washington,
DC: Regnery Publishing,
2004), viii.

44 Stanton and Maier, 22.

46 *Loving v. Virginia*, 388 U.S.
1 (1967), available online
at "US Supreme Court
Center," *Justia.com*, 2005,
http://supreme.justia.com
/us/388/1/case.html
(November 7, 2007).

48 Sprigg., 66.

48 Stanton and Maier, 27.

49 Robert M. Baird and
Stuart E. Rosenbaum,
eds., *Same-Sex Marriage:
The Moral and Legal Debate*
(New York: Prometheus
Books, 1997), 109.

49 Ibid.

51 Stanton and Maier, 55.

51–52 Ibid.

51 Kotulski, 107.

52–53 Stanton and Maier, 57–58.

53 Andrew Sullivan, *Virtually Normal: An Argument about Homosexuality* (New York: Knopf, 1995), 171, 178–179, 185.

54 Myers and Scanzoni, 126.

55 Ibid., 27–29.

55 Stanton and Maier., 119.

57 Ibid., 35.

61 Evan Wolfson, *Why Marriage Matters: America, Equality, and Gay People's Right to Marry* (New York: Simon & Schuster, 2004), 5.

65 Baird and Rosenbaum, 108, 112.

67 Jonathan Rauch, *Gay Marriage: Why It Is Good for Gays, Good for Straights, Good for America* (New York: Henry Holt, 2004), 49.

67 Myers and Scanzoni, 127.

67 Baird and Rosenbaum, 165.

68 Sullivan, 181–182.

68 Chauncey, 129.

69 Evan Gerstmann, *Same-Sex Marriage and the Constitution* (New York: Cambridge University Press, 2004), 200.

74 FRC, *The Vision and the Work of Family Research Council,* pamphlet mailed to author by the FRC, 1998.

75 Jennifer M. Lehmann, ed., *The Gay and Lesbian Marriage and Family Reader: Analyses of Problems and Prospects for the 21st Century* (New York: Richard Altschuler and Associates, 2001), 281.

75 *New York Times,* June 18, 1998.

75 Ibid.

77 Wolfson, 93–94.

79 Sprigg, 101.

79 Ibid.

79 Wolfson, 85.

79–80 Stanton and Maier, 112–117, 119–120.

81 Wolfson, 42.

81 Ibid., 92–93.

84 Wolfson, 32.

84 Baird and Rosenbaum, 230

86 Baird and Rosenbaum, 206–210.

87 Wolfson, 46.

87 Ibid., 49.

86–87 Nancy F. Cott, *Public Vows: A History of Marriage and the Nation* (Cambridge, MA: Harvard University Press, 2000), 216–217.

90 Wolfson, 34.

91 Ibid., 43.

91 Baird and Rosenbaum, 21–22.

92 Ibid., 232.

92 David Moats, *Civil War: A Battle for Gay Marriage* (New York: Harcourt, 2004), 11.

92 Ibid., 31, 34.

92–93 Ibid., 11.

93 Ibid., 30.

93 Ibid., 199.

97 Ibid., 232.

101 Ibid., 265.

100 Baird and Rosenbaum, 188.

100 Michael Mello, *Legalizing Gay Marriage* (Philadelphia: Temple University Press, 2004), 7–8.

100–101 Chauncey, 65.

103 Wolfson, 140–141.

102 Moats, 263.

104 Senator Wayne Allard, "S. J. Res. 30 [108th]: Marriage resolution," March 22, 2004, available online at *GovTrack.us*, http://www.govtrack.us/congress/billtext.xpd?bill=sj108-30 (November 11, 2007).

110 Moats, 266.

110 Sprigg, 20.

110 Wolfson, 26.

110 Rauch, 104.

108 Chauncey, 143–144.

112 Sprigg, 69.

112 Chauncey, 129.

112 Myers and Scanzoni, 126.

SELECTED BIBLIOGRAPHY

Alliance Defense Fund. "Doma Watch: Your Legal Source for Defense of Marriage Acts Information." *DOMAwatch.org.* 2006. http://www.domawatch.org (November 6, 2007).

Baird, Robert M., and Stuart E. Rosenbaum, eds. *Same-Sex Marriage: The Moral and Legal Debate.* Amherst, NY: Prometheus Books, 1997.

Chauncey, George. *Why Marriage? The History Shaping Today's Debate over Gay Equality.* New York: Basic Books, 2004.

Cott, Nancy F. *Public Vows: A History of Marriage and the Nation.* Cambridge, MA: Harvard University Press, 2000.

Dworkin, Ronald. "Three Questions for America." *New York Review of Books* 52, no. 14, September 21, 2006, PAGES TK.

Eskridge, William N., Jr. *The Case for Same-Sex Marriage: From Sexual Liberty to Civilized Commitment.* New York: Free Press, 1996.

Gerstmann, Evan. *Same-Sex Marriage and the Constitution.* New York: Cambridge University Press, 2004.

GovTrack.us. "Tracking the 110th United States Congress." *GovTrack.us.* 2007. http://www.govtrack.us (November 6, 2007).

Kotulski, Davina. *Why You Should Give a Damn about Gay Marriage.* Los Angeles: Advocate Books, 2004.

Lehmann, Jennifer M., ed. *The Gay and Lesbian Marriage and Family Reader: Analyses of Problems and Prospects for the 21st Century.* New York: Richard Altschuler and Associates, 2001.

Mello, Michael. *Legalizing Gay Marriage*. Philadelphia: Temple University Press, 2004.

Moats, David. *Civil Wars: A Battle for Gay Marriage*. New York: Harcourt, 2004.

Mohr, Richard D. *The Long Arc of Justice: Lesbian and Gay Marriage, Equality, and Rights*. New York: Columbia University Press, 2005.

Myers, David G., and Letha Dawson Scanzoni. *What God Has Joined Together? A Christian Case for Gay Marriage*. New York: HarperCollins, 2005.

National Conference of State Legislatures: The Forum for America's Ideas. "Same-Sex Marriage Timeline." *National Conference of State Legislatures*. October 15, 2007. http://www.ncsl.org/programs/cyf/samesextime.htm (November 6, 2007).

Rauch, Jonathan. *Gay Marriage: Why It Is Good for Gays, Good for Straights, Good for America*. New York: Henry Holt, 2004.

Religious Newswriters Foundation. *ReligionLink*. 2007. http://www.religionlink.org (November 6, 2007).

Rennert, Amy, ed. *We Do: A Celebration of Gay and Lesbian Marriage*. Foreword by Gavin Newsom. San Francisco: Chronicle Books, 2004.

Sprigg, Peter. *Outrage: How Gay Activists and Liberal Judges Are Trashing Democracy to Redefine Marriage*. Washington, DC: Regnery Publishing, 2004.

Stanton, Glenn T., and Bill Maier. *Marriage on Trial: The Case against Same-Sex Marriage and Parenting.* Downers Grove, IL: Intervarsity Press, 2004.

Sullivan, Andrew. *Virtually Normal: An Argument about Homosexuality.* New York: Knopf, 1995.

Wolfson, Evan. *Why Marriage Matters: America, Equality, and Gay People's Right to Marry.* New York: Simon & Schuster, 2004.

FURTHER READING AND WEBSITES

BOOKS

Burns, Kate, ed. *Gay Marriage*. Detroit: Greenhaven Press, 2005.

Dobson, James. *Marriage Under Fire: Why We Must Win This War*. Wheaton, IL: Tyndale House Publishers, 2007.

Ellison, Marvin Mahan. *Same-Sex Marriage?: A Christian Ethical Analysis*. Cleveland: Pilgrim Press, 2004.

Garner, Abigail. *Families Like Mine: Children of Gay Parents Tell It Like It Is*. New York: HarperCollins, 2004.

Kafka, Tina. *Gay Rights*. San Diego: Lucent Books, 2005.

Koppelman, Andrew. *Same Sex, Different States: When Same-Sex Marriages Cross State Lines*. New Haven, CT: Yale University Press, 2006.

Snow, Judith E. *How It Feels to Have a Gay or Lesbian Parent: A Book by Kids for Kids of All Ages*. New York: Haworth Press, 2004.

Stockland, Patricia M. *Essential Viewpoints: Same-Sex Marriage*. Edina, MN: ABDO Publishing Company, 2007.

WEBSITES

BBC—Religion and Ethics—Same-Sex Marriage
http://www.bbc.co.uk/religion/ethics/samesexmarriage/index.shtml
This site from the BBC provides a look at the arguments on both sides of the gay marriage debate.

Catholic Answers Special Report: Gay Marriage
http://www.catholic.com/library/gay_marriage.asp
This page offers a thorough and thoughtful explanation of the
Catholic Church's position on same-sex marriage, as well as the
theological and sociological reasoning behind this position.

HRC—Marriage & Relationship Recognition
http://www.hrc.org/issues/marriage.asp
This pro-same-sex-marriage page, run by the Human Rights
Campaign, features the latest news on the issue in the United
States. It also has listings and explanations of various laws relat-
ing to same-sex marriage in different states and stories and
statements from people involved in the debate.

Law/Civil Rights at PollingReport.com
http://www.pollingreport.com/civil.htm
This site provides the results of recent polls on the subject of laws
and civil rights, including polls on gay marriage. These polls are
all taken from a variety of major news sources and often provide
comparisons with previous polls on the same subject to show
how opinions have changed.

The Pew Forum on Religion & Public Life: Gay Marriage
http://pewforum.org/gay-marriage/
The Pew Forum, a nonpartisan site, provides a listing of the
most recent articles on gay marriage from publications around
the United States.

RESOURCES TO CONTACT

Alliance for Marriage
PO Box 2490
Merrifield, VA 22116
http://www.allianceformarriage.org
The website for this nonprofit organization states its goals and mission, to defend traditional marriage, and provides links for further information.

Concerned Women for America
1015 Fifteenth Street NW, Suite 1100
Washington, DC 20005
http://www.cwfa.org/hot-topics.asp#marriage
This website offers links to sites promoting the defense and protection of the traditional definition of marriage.

Family Research Council
801 G Street NW
Washington, DC 20001
http://www.protectmarriage.org
The Family Research Council site has links to resources for researching a marriage protection amendment.

Focus on the Family
Colorado Springs, CO 80995
http://www.family.org
This website contains articles, links, and other resources addressing marriage, faith, social issues, and other life challenges.

Freedom to Marry
116 West 23rd Street, Suite 500
New York, NY 10011
http://www.freedomtomarry.org
This site has true stories, news articles, and information on how to get involved in the fight for marriage equality.

Human Rights Campaign
1640 Rhode Island Avenue NW
Washington, DC 20036-3278
http://www.hrc.org
The Human Rights Campaign site provides information on the fight for equal rights for all citizens and suggestions on how to get involved.

Institute for Marriage and Public Policy
PO Box 1231
Manassas, VA 20108
http://www.marriagedebate.com
This website offers access to a wide variety of articles and links on all things marriage, from same-sex marriage to divorce law reform.

Lambda Legal Defense and Education Fund
National Headquarters
120 Wall Street, Suite 1500
New York, NY 10005-3904
http://www.lambdalegal.org
This site gives information on Lambda Legal's work to achieve equal civil rights for gay, lesbian, bisexual, and transgender people as well as those with HIV.

National Center for Lesbian Rights (NCLR)
Marriage and Family Law Project
NCLR National Office
780 Market Street, Suite 370
San Francisco, CA 94102
http://www.nclrights.org/site/PageServer?pagename=issue_families
This NCLR website gives information on the center's work to keep parents and their gay, lesbian, bisexual, and transgender children together. The site lists links to news articles documenting NCLR's work.

National Gay and Lesbian Task Force
1325 Massachusetts Avenue NW, Suite 600
Washington, DC 20005
http://www.thetaskforce.org
The task force's website discusses a variety of issues, including same-sex marriage and parenting, provides access to reports and research, and has links to events across the country.

Pew Forum on Religion and Public Life
1615 L Street NW, Suite 700
Washington, DC 20036-5610
http://www.pewforum.org/gay-marriage/
This site offers a variety of resources looking into the religious perspective on gay marriage.

INDEX

ABOUT THE AUTHOR

TRICIA ANDRYSZEWSKI writes on a variety of topics for both elementary children and young adults. Her numerous books include *Terrorism in America, School Prayer: A History of the Debate, Gay Rights, Abortion, Walking the Earth: The History of Human Migration,* and *Mass Extinction: Examining the Current Crisis.*

PHOTO ACKNOWLEDGMENTS